The Henleaze Book

Veronica Bowerman

D1614728

First published in 1991
Fully revised and expanded in 2006

© Veronica Bowerman 2006

email: henleazebook@yahoo.co.uk

ISBN 10: 0-9553567-0-9
ISBN 13: 978-0-9553567-0-4

This book is sold subject to the condition that it shall not, by way of trade or otherwise, be lent, resold, hired out, or otherwise circulated without the publisher's prior consent in any form of binding or cover other than that in which it is published and without a similar condition including this condition being imposed on the subsequent publisher.

The moral right of Veronica Bowerman has been asserted in accordance with the Copyright, Designs And Patents Act 1988.

NOTICE TO READERS
While great care has been taken to ensure that the information in this publication is accurate, Veronica Bowerman cannot accept responsibility for any error or omission that may have occurred. It is sold, therefore, on the condition that neither the Compiler nor Editors can be held legally responsible for the consequences of any error or omission there may be.

We welcome comments, suggestions and feedback from readers and users of this book which could help with any possible future editions.

Published by Redcliffe Press Ltd, Bristol
Typeset by Harper Phototypesetters Ltd, Northampton
Cover design by eandp, Bath www.eandp.co.uk
Printed by Gutenberg Press, Malta

The paper used in this book is from a mill which has FSC Accreditation
(i.e. their wood pulp comes from managed forests and is acid free).

CONTENTS

ACKNOWLEDGEMENTS

I would like to thank the Henleaze Society Committee of 1991, in particular, Ron Lyne, Sylvia Kelly and Elizabeth Herring; without their help the first edition of *The Henleaze Book* would never have been completed!

Many past and present residents were interviewed for the first edition; a few minor mistakes highlighted by readers have been corrected for this edition. Since 1991, I have received additional information including photographs, plans and other memorabilia and would like to thank all these people for this as well as for their generous time and enthusiasm.

For this second edition I would also like to highlight the support once again given by Sylvia Kelly as well as Maureen Jones and Caroline Sparks for their proofreading assistance. Two other friends of special mention who also have a unique knowledge of the Henleaze area are Ray Pepworth and Mike Brooks who both gave me unrestricted access to their collections of documents and photographs.

Veronica Bowerman
September 2006

Copyright information

Photographs, maps and plans

Many thanks to all concerned for permission to reprint copyright material – each has been individually acknowledged on the respective pages.

Advertisers and sponsors

The following advertisers and sponsors have assisted in partly financing this publication:

ADVERTISERS (more details in their respective advertisements)
AMD Solicitors
C J Hole
Henleaze Dental Practice
Red Maids' School
Your Move

SPONSORS (further details in Part 7 – Henleaze Road Businesses)

AMD Solicitors	Solicitors	100 Henleaze Road	0117 962 1205
C J Hole	Estate Agent	108 Henleaze Road	0117 962 9221
Newsom & Davies	Optician	45 Henleaze Road	0117 962 2612
Whirlwind Videos	DVD & Video Hire	41 Henleaze Road	0117 962 4965

Many thanks to you all for providing this invaluable support.

CJ HOLE .com
est. 1867

The No. 1
LOCAL AGENT

All properties marketed on all major internet sites with virtual tours, walk through tours and floor plans

Guaranteed colour advertising in the Bristol Evening Post

All viewings accompanied by a member of our experienced staff

Opening doors in Bristol for over 3 centuries!

A reputation built on success!

For your *free valuation* **call**
Henleaze Office on 962 9221 or
Bishopston Office on 923 2888

OPEN:	9am – 7pm	Monday to Friday
	9am – 5pm	Saturdays

Ombudsman
www.oea.co.uk

www.cjhole.co.uk

Advice Making a Difference

Telephone us on (0117) 9621205 or
visit our website **www.amdsolicitors.com**

- Commercial and residential conveyancing

- Starting up or buying and selling a business

- Wills and trusts

- Personal tax and estate planning

- Family and matrimonial law

Our three offices at Westbury Park, Henleaze and Shirehampton all offer free on street or forecourt parking

Our specialist solicitors are part of the network of **Lawyers For Your Business,** panel members of The Society of Tax and Estate Practitioners, The Law Society Family Law Panel and accredited by the Solicitors Family Law Association

HENLEAZE DENTAL PRACTICE

- *Preventative Care*
- *Cosmetic Treatment*
- *Crown & Bridgework*

- *Evening & Saturday Appts.*
- *Friendly, Caring Staff*
- *Emergency Service*

Dr Mark Haseltine, B.D.S.
Dr Susan Lavington, B.D.S.

130 Henleaze Road, Henleaze, BS9 4LB

Tel: 0117 962 0534

www.henleazedental.co.uk

Denplan

The Red Maids' School
Westbury-on-Trym
11-18 *education for girls*

16 34

We encourage every girl to discover and develop
her own abilities. We look forward to meeting you.

Westbury-on-Trym Bristol BS9 3AW
Telephone 0117 962 2641 www.redmaids.bristol.sch.uk

PART 1
INTRODUCTION

Overview

Henleaze is a small residential area in North Bristol bounded by Kellaway Avenue and Wellington Hill West, with a more indefinite boundary along Westbury Road and North View.

Why Henleaze? The reader can choose the erudite explanation of its Anglo Saxon connotation as 'The Place of the Wild Bird Wood' or 'High Meadows', or alternatively select the answer that it was named after one Robert Henley who was in possession of much of the land in the area in 1659.

Henleaze cannot boast of any real depth of history. Although it is largely built on a high point of land around 400 feet (122 metres) with extensive views it has no strategic position in relation to defence. It appears to have been shunned by both the Ancient Britons and Romans as a place to build either earthworks or redoubts. However since the first edition we have learned a small bronze figurine of the god Mercury, only about two inches (five centimetres) high, dated around 150AD was found on Golden Hill. The Archaeology Department of Bristol Museum advise that there are no records of any building or development on Golden Hill during the Roman occupation.

Figurine of the god Mercury
Found on Golden Hill in the 1930s and thought to have been used by the Romans for altar decoration. Approximately 2,200 years old, 5 centimetres high and made of copper alloy. (*Bowerman photo collection, courtesy of the Bristol Museum*)

Residents of Henleaze are therefore very unlikely to discover any ancient artefacts when digging their gardens. The ground is not completely uninteresting for there are many fossils – sea fern, shells, ammonites, trilobites etc. from the days when the land was shallows under the sea some 200–500 million years ago and turned into limestone rock.

The geological assessment of Henleaze is that the area demonstrates a clay sub-soil streaked with sedimentary rock. The bands of clay/rock are quite narrow and often not more than a few centimetres deep. There is no granite beneath the surface to fuel concern about radon gas; neither are there any known coal seams under Henleaze, the working of which always gives rise to thoughts of subsidence. However, the clay does heave in the winter months and this routine change of volume can encourage hairline cracks in the walls and render of buildings. Limestone was quarried and burnt with coal in a brick or stone built kiln to produce lime. Five lime kilns were originally in the area; three at the Eastfield Quarry – two still exist there in Clark's yard – and two at Southmead Quarry, one of which was demolished in the 1930s to make way for Henleaze Swimming Club.

We have no evidence to show whether the product was for general use (for example fertiliser or bird lime) but a good guess would be that most of it was used in mortar in the house building expansion of the 1800s, specifically the development of Horfield and Redland.

There is a further feature of interest – a small band of zinc/lead sulphide ore that climbs towards the surface somewhere near the Eastfield Inn. The zinc/lead sulphides look a green/grey colour, but they are too far below the surface for any gardener to unearth them. The ore-body in Henleaze is almost the end or tail of the large seam that the Romans worked in the Mendips which provided much of the lead products used locally (for example in the lead water pipes in Roman baths). At the Henleaze end some enterprising individuals evidently did a little bit of mining, driving a sloping tunnel (an adit mine) from the bottom of the quarry on the Henleaze side of Waters Lane. The mineshaft extends some way underground and since the quarry pre-dates the entrance to the mine, we might guess that perhaps the quarrymen carried out this additional mining for perks. Further, they had all the materials on site – coal and clay in the quarry – to smelt the ore into saleable lead. The process is very simple – it has been commonly used for more than 4,000 years – and it would have been a logical step.

In the 1500s Henleaze formed part of the Manor of Westbury-on-Trym which, until 1544, belonged to the College of Westbury. In that year the Dean ceded the College and its possessions to King Henry VIII, who in turn granted it to Sir Ralph Sadleir, one of his famous courtiers.

The Manor remained in the possession of the Sadleir family for over 100 years.

In 1659 Ralph Sadleir's grandson, Ralph, sold a property in Henleaze with 35 acres (14 hectares) of land to Robert Henley for £540. It was then known as Henley's House and later on Henleaze Park and St Margaret's School.

In the 1800s Henleaze was still very rural, mainly meadows where cattle were grazed and some arable land was cultivated by the local farmers. Landowners also established orchards to provide fruit and wine. Henleaze Road was then known as Henleaze Lane and nicknamed Endless Lane by the locals.

The 1841 Tithe Map shows Henley House, Henley Grove and Springfield as the three main residences in Henleaze. Claremont was not built until 1851 and is in fact the only remaining gentleman's residence still standing in Henleaze. It is currently used as a special school by Bristol City Council. Some other major residences adjacent to Henleaze such as Burfield House, Westmead, Southmead Manor, Burfield Priory and Waterdale House have also been included in this book to give a better overview of the area.

Tithe map of Henleaze, 1841 *(enhanced by Harold A Lane)*

3

It is interesting to note the following 2006 statistics from Lloyds TSB, one of the two remaining banks in Henleaze: 'We have 12 customers over 90 years old and two over 100.' *Editor's note: Henleaze must be a healthy place!* We hope you will enjoy this book.

Editor's note: The original 1991 introduction was compiled by Ron Lyne, Chairman (1991–93) and President of The Henleaze Society (1994–2002). This has been edited and updated for the second edition by Veronica Bowerman and Sylvia Kelly.

2001 Census

Henleaze Ward consists broadly of Henleaze and most of Westbury Park. The boundary of the ward is Wellington Hill West, Kellaway Avenue, Coldharbour Road, Belvedere Road, Claypit Road, Westbury Road, Priory Avenue, Eastfield and Eastfield Road.

Aerial view, 1930s, (taken before Northumbria Drive was built in the late 1930s). Note the First World War allotments in the centre. The following buildings are quite clearly shown before their demolition: Northumberland House School, 1937: The Priory 1938: Waterdale House, 1960s: Henley Park Grove Mansion, 1967 and the Royal Blind School, 1971. (*Peter Davey collection*)

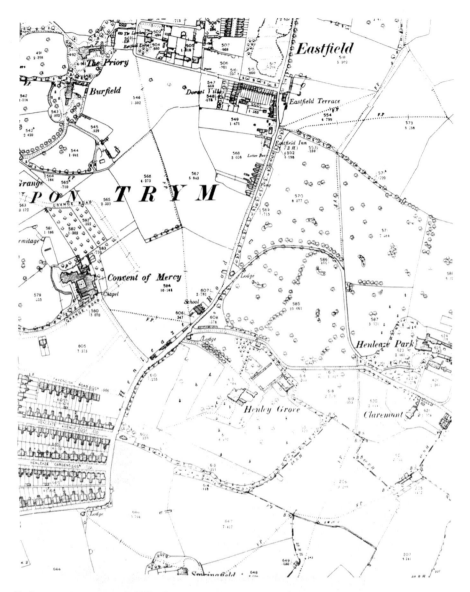

Ordnance survey map of Henleaze, 1903

Historical dates for Henleaze

Up to Fifth Century	Roman Occupation of Britain	The Romans left in the Fifth Century AD. A Roman figurine found on Golden Hill is now in the Bristol Museum.
1319	Manor House	Original Manor House built on the present Southmead Road site.
1539	Manor House	It was by then the property of the Nunnery of St Mary Magdalene. It was one of the first to be disbanded by Henry VIII.
1659	Henley's House	Built for Robert Henley. A subsequent building here known as St Margaret's School was demolished in the 1960s.
1700s	Clark's Cottage	Built for the owners of Eastfield and Southmead quarries.
1727	18 Henleaze Rd (near Downs Park East)	The oldest Lodge in Henleaze; originally built for Springfield House.
1810 approx	166 Henleaze Rd (by Wanscow Walk)	Thatched lodge cottage, similar to the ones at Blaise Hamlet.
1820	Westmead House	Sir Edward Protheroe built this for his Mother *(now St Ursula's High School)*.
1820	Springfield House	Subsequently demolished in 1937. Roads now on the site include Fallodon Way and Wildcroft Road.
1820s	Eastfield	Building started here, including Eastfield Lodge and The Larches.

1841	Tithe Map	First known map of the area shows Henley House, Henley Grove and Springfield as the three main residences in Henleaze.
1851–3	Claremont House	Built and since the 1950s run as Claremont School.
1903	URC	Church completed and now known as Trinity-Henleaze United Reformed Church.
1905	Lloyds – fishmonger	First shop in Henleaze.
1911	Royal School for the Blind	Purpose-built school opened, demolished in 1971.
1916	Eastfield and Southmead Quarries	Ceased working.
1916	Henleaze Lane renamed Henleaze Road	Walking wounded soldiers from the Battle of the Somme made their way to Southmead Hospital along this Lane.
1919	Henleaze Swimming Club	Founded, still running and located in Lake Road.
1926	St Peter's Church	Foundation stone laid.
1930s	Aerial maps	First known showing Henleaze.
1973	The Henleaze Society	Formed and in 2005 had a membership of 1,400 households in the area.
1990	Henleaze Exhibition Arts/Crafts	The first one was held in St Ursula's High School.
1991	Henleaze Book	First edition with a 1,500 print run was sold out by Christmas.

1992	Henleaze Concerts	The first one was held in the URC, Waterford Road.
1993	Golden Hill	Tesco supermarket built after a long battle with protestors. This made central government look very carefully at greenfield sites.
2002	The Henleaze Society	An Environmental Award from Bristol Civic Society was received by the Society for enhancing the environment, particularly Old Quarry Park.

LOCAL BUILDERS

Editor's note:
Many builders have helped make Henleaze the unique place that it is today.
However here are some who actually lived AND worked in Henleaze.

Charles H. Reed

Charles H. Reed, Builder and Contractor, assisted Frank Wilkins from Wilkins & Coventry on new properties in the mid-1920s in Antrim Road as well as parts of Brecon and Waterford Roads. In 1926 Charles Reed lived with his family in 135 Henleaze Road, a house he had built himself. The land was given to Mr Reed by Mr Wilkins as a wedding present. Henleaze Road was not numbered then so the house was initially called Gwenchas after Gwen and Charles Reed. The property, situated next door to the church, was often mistaken for the Manse.

The Voke Family

The Voke family of builders had a huge impact on the design of Henleaze in the 1920s and 1930s.

John Henry Voke was the first of the building Vokes in Bristol. He was born around 1850 and had 14 children. He lived and built many properties in the Bedminster area.

Second generation, William John Voke was born in 1874 and was originally an ornamental plasterer by trade. He travelled to Africa in his early twenties and was responsible for the rococo work in the Court Rooms of Bulawayo in Zimbabwe. The money he made from that job enabled him to start up building in Bedminster and subsequently in Redland and Cranbrook Road areas before 1914. He bought a farm in the Henleaze area and started building there as well. William John was responsible for building the shops on Henleaze Road, from Lloyds TSB to St Peter's Hospice shop, as well as the block in Wellington Hill West containing a post office at one end and a hairdresser at the other. Residential builds in Henleaze included houses in Grange Court Road, Brecon Road, Hill View, Rockside Drive, Oakwood Road, Grange Park and Henleaze Park Drive.

Third generation, Leon John Voke was born in 1913 and by his early 20s was in partnership with his father William John. In the Henleaze area they were responsible for the building of houses in Lakewood Crescent,

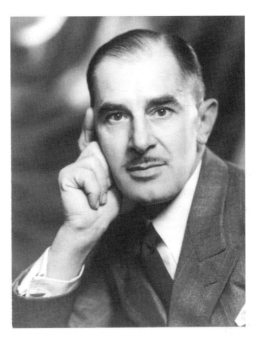

Ivor Voke, *c*1930
Ivor was the family architect and designed many houses for Henleaze. His office was in the rear of the Voke building office at 103 Henleaze Road (now Treasures). (*Voke family collection*)

Lakewood Road and in Grange Park; the houses on the west side of Grange Park – those with odd numbers – are predominately 1930 properties and were built by Leon John while those on the east side predominately date to the 1920s and were built by William John. The original occupants of Grange Park were a Who's Who of businesses in Bristol at that time.

Ivor Voke was born in 1905. He designed, and the Voke family built, a wide range of housing from the very small to the luxury bespoke, which was not the norm at the time. Ivor started his practice in the late 1920s and continued until the early 1960s. His hand-drawn coloured plans are a delight to see. It took him a Saturday morning to design a small house but a bespoke large home could take up to a fortnight. As part of his training he was required to draw various pieces of classical architecture including a Corinthian capital and base.

Between the two World Wars in Bristol there were many small builders and four large builders. Two of the large builders operated in the south of the city and two, Stride and Voke, operated in the north. During World War II the needs of the military effectively put an end to house building and after there were many restrictions on building materials, for example it could take approximately two years to requisition a bath!

The fourth generation of this building family is Conrad Voke, one of seven brothers. He started building in 1986 but has concentrated on renovations, restorations, repairs and extensions in place of new builds.

Leonard Watts

Leonard Watts (1897–1963) was born in Bishopston and was one of a family of ten children. He lied about his age and served with the Somerset Light Yeomanry in the First World War. He was wounded, but survived to become an apprentice plumber with his uncle. After about five years of apprenticeship he arrived five minutes late for work one day and was locked out. He then decided that would be the last time he worked there and so changed direction.

Using his hard-earned savings he contacted people in Bishopston where he was well-known and a member of the church of St Michael's and All Angels on Pigsty Hill. He started off by offering to install lavatories in houses, but by the mid-1930s he was responsible for building the Kingshill Estate in Dursley. The estate was described as one of the most magnificent sites in the country and properties were available to all to rent or buy.

Cheriton Place, 1934
Len Watts, a builder and local resident, built these and several other semis in Cheriton Place in the 1930s. Number 52 with SOLD written across the windows. The sun pattern across the top of the porch is still there in 2006. (*Watts' family collection*)

In 1934 Len Watts built houses in Henleaze, four semi-detached properties in Cheriton Place, one of which (no. 52) was sold for £130 at the time. He also built a terrace in Russell Grove.

The Watts family lived in 25 Henleaze Gardens from 1944, but moved to a Voke's home, 18 Brecon Road, in the early 1960s. Len had always admired Voke's houses. It was interesting to view the Chappell and Matthews catalogue of the chattels that were on sale in 1944. Len bought many of the items – there were 676 in all! He pencilled in the prices of the items he had purchased in the catalogue which included:

Linoleum as laid on top landing – 10 shillings (50p)
Folding easy chair upholstered in brown plush – £7-5s-0d (£7.25)
Engraved copper warming pan – £3-17s-6d (£3.87)
Black out curtains – 20 shillings per pair (£1)
A superior Axminster stair carpet – £27

By the start of World War II Len Watts was employing 300 men but all building work stopped when war started. Len's wife, Olive Watts was a Colonel in the local Red Cross. Len was too old for the war service but he helped Olive and was able to be an air-raid warden as well. They were fortunate having an income from the estate and were able to devote themselves to war effort.

Len, as he was known, had left school at a very early age and regretted his lack of a full education so he was determined, and ensured, that all four of his children had the benefit of a good education. He was self-made, but a very kind and generous man, a devout Christian who was loved by many people from all backgrounds.

PART 2
LARGE HOUSES

Burfield House

The house appears to have been built in the early 1800s. Residents included E. B. Fripp in 1825, Edwards Bowles, soap manufacturer, in 1838 and John Robinson in 1849. In June 1877 Burfield House and its estate of 15 acres (six hectares) was sold to Mr Symes for £8,050. It appears that Mr Symes became Sir Robert Symes who then sold the house to Red Maids' School in 1911. There were two lodges at each drive entrance and these survive today *(see also further information under Schools)*.

Burfield Priory (The Priory)

This interesting property was situated next to Burfield House and marked on the 1841 Tithe Map. It was demolished to make way for Priory Court Road.

Burfield Priory (The Priory), c1915
Set in 17 acres, complete with look-out tower. The grounds and house were auctioned in 1938. The house was subsequently demolished and replaced by the houses in the new roads – Priory Avenue and Priory Court Road – created at that time. (*Mike Brooks collection*)

Occupants/owners include the following:

- 1849 William Boyd
- 1871 James Lucas, age 45, and three maiden sisters in their fifties
- 1880 Misses Lucas
- 1895 Rev G. F. Whidbourne. (The 1900 map of the area suggests that he owned a large area of land as far as the side of Henleaze Road looking north.)

In the 1920s summer garden parties were held at the Priory with crowds of people and music which went on into the night, keeping the Red Maids' next door awake in their dormitories. The girls were thrilled to hear the rich contralto voice of Dame Clara Butt on one occasion singing *Land of Hope and Glory* followed by the National Anthem.

After William Henry Butler J.P. died, the Priory Estate was auctioned on 10 March 1938 by Lalonde Bros & Parham at the Grand Hotel, Bristol. There were 17 acres (seven hectares) containing a Gothic design mansion,

The Priory Estate, 1938
17 acres containing a Gothic design mansion, two lodges, farm buildings and garages were auctioned on 10 March 1938 by Lalonde Bros & Parham at the Grand Hotel, Bristol. (*Mike Brooks collection*)

two lodges, farm buildings, garages, lawns, pastures and well-timbered grounds.

A summary of the accommodation arranged on three floors in the Mansion was: Gothic entrance hall, 12 bedrooms and dressing rooms, four reception rooms, three bathrooms, kitchens, servants' hall and usual offices. In 1938 the property was fitted with electric light, central heating and hot water circulation from independent boilers. A spiral staircase from the second floor led to a look out tower on the south side.

Red Maids' school and its grounds were adjoining this estate but their Governors were not prepared to buy the whole of the Priory estate and then sell off what they did not need. The Priory estate was subsequently sold for £18,600 to a local builder in 1938. The school found that they were then unable to buy part of the land for a playing field or even the belt of trees alongside their new drive. The Priory and its buildings were demolished and replaced by the houses in the new roads Priory Avenue and Priory Court Road.

Claremont House

It is not known who commissioned the house to be built but building started in 1851 and was completed in 1853. The grounds were then bounded by the present Kellaway Avenue, Park Grove and Springfield Grove. The gardens were extremely large extending to the present Henleaze Park and Park Grove junctions.

The original name may have been Havelock Villa but this was changed to Havelock House when occupied by Henry W. Green from 1865 to 1868 with his wife, Elizabeth and one child.

In 1873 Charles Abbot Peters and his family moved into the house. He had been living at 117 Pembroke Road in a house called 'Claremont' so again the name was changed. Charles Peters was an attorney and solicitor with the firm of Hobbs Peters and Co. in Corn Street. When his wife Kate died in 1884, Charles moved to Herbert Lodge in Cotham Park.

The next occupants were Thomas Macaulay Miller and his wife, Julia Mary George (from the famous brewing family). Thomas died in 1894 and Mrs Miller continued to own the property until August 1898 when it was sold at auction. From the sale particulars we know that Claremont was a substantial house set in 11 acres (four and a half hectares), with glasshouses and a conservatory. The interior included a dining room, drawing room, morning room (complete with telephone to the stables), downstairs cloakrooms with hot and cold water, kitchens, larders and also beer and wine cellars. Upstairs were seven bedrooms and two dressing rooms, and a bathroom with hot and cold water. The sale particulars also stressed that the property had benefited from a large expenditure on drainage 'which is believed to be perfect.'

'The stabling and Gardener's cottage have recently been erected and are in perfect order.' (Sale particulars 1898) There was a partly covered paved yard, and a second coach house with scullery and WC adjoining and two rooms over for the coachman. The cottage adjoining the stable contained a sitting room, kitchen, larder, three bedrooms and offices and had a separate garden. Badminton hounds also used to hunt the district.

The house was bought by Caleb Bruce-Cole for £9000, well over the estimate of £6000 – £7000. He came to live there with his wife Edith and their children. In 1886, 24-year-old Caleb Bruce-Cole paid £950 – a loan from his father – to buy out the chocolate manufacturers, H. J. Packer & Co, based in St Paul's. It then took five years for the business to come into profit but within the next five years more space was needed. Caleb's brother, Horace joined him and the site at Greenbank was purchased. Three blocks, planned largely by Horace, were to an ultra-modern design. All corners inside were rounded so that dust was not trapped and new sprinkler systems were incorporated. Horace died before the new factory was opened in 1901. The move from St Paul's was carried out in stages and the premises there finally closed in 1902. The business grew steadily and between 1903 and 1912 sales increased by 250 per cent. More investment capital was raised in 1908 when the firm became a limited company. Caleb used to cycle to the factory from Henleaze wearing a long jacket, plus fours and a bowler hat. Sadly the factory, now known as Elizabeth Shaw, is due for closure in 2007.

The Bruce-Cole family used to holiday every year in Evancoed, Wales in the early 1900s. They journeyed by train and took their usual entourage of servants with the family and guests as well as cows, chickens and various pets. Mr Bruce-Cole ensured that the train advertised 'Packer's Chocolates' on the sides of the van that accommodated the animals.

The cowman had a herd of six Jersey cows that grazed in the field adjacent to Springfield Grove – now the site of Henleaze Junior School. Cook put their milk into pans within vats daily to make clotted cream and the residents of Golden Hill and Kellaway Avenue came to the house for the buttermilk. Mr Poultney, the butcher in Henleaze Road, used to kill the calves at Claremont with a poleaxe and sell the meat in his shop.

The area was well known for red foxes, supposedly different from today's grey urban fox. A large pond was drained into a culvert along Springfield Grove.

Caleb Bruce-Cole added a south wing to Claremont in 1909. Although he died in 1912 his wife continued with the building work and in 1913 she doubled the size of the garage (next to Claremont Lodge) so that it would accommodate two motor cars and have an inspection pit with a tin for collecting oil.

In the 1920s two sisters were employed as live-in maids. At that time 90% of the houses in Henleaze had country girls as live-in maids who were paid approximately £3 per month. Before her marriage, in the late 1920s, Mrs Meek and her sister, who was the parlour maid, had a large bedroom with their own adjacent bathroom. They used to rise at 7am daily. Mrs Bruce-Cole, the family and visitors were always brought tea in bed. Mrs Meek used to clean the large hall which contained lots of brassware and several decorative bed warmers. After breakfast the other rooms were cleaned and the housework was usually finished by midday, except for washing up after meals. Mrs Meek was required to sew, mainly mending, but this apparently did not amount to much. She used to have one half-day off a week and alternate Sundays. Most days she used to take the dogs, a Sealyham and a Scotch terrier nicknamed 'Black and White Whisky' for walks in the then rural surroundings.

As parlour maid, Mrs Meek's sister used to lay the tables and wait at meals. She used to answer the telephone and assist Mrs Bruce-Cole with the paperwork required for running Claremont. The dining room was one of the most attractive rooms in the house. The walls were panelled in mahogany, just stopping a foot short of the ceiling. The huge dining table was always used for meals, even if it was only dinner for one – a solitary place would be laid at one end. Mrs Bruce-Cole enjoyed entertaining. It was normal for six courses: soup, fish, meat, sweet, cheese and fruit. Finger bowls were supplied and the appropriate wines were served with each course.

The Bruce-Cole family used to hold an annual fete in one of their fields each year for St Peter's Church.

Claremont Lodge and Cottage were the homes of the chauffeur and gardener. The chauffeur enjoyed driving the large yellow Buick. There was a large walled fruit garden where St Margaret's Drive now stands, by the wall bordering Kenton Mews. The gardener grew nectarines and peaches, all beautifully trained against the wall. There was a huge bed of strawberries and a large vine in the massive greenhouse which was demolished when St Margaret's Drive was built in the 1960s. Mrs Bruce-Cole let a large part of the garden grow wild. Relatives and friends stayed most weekends and many of them used to help find sticks in the wild part of the garden for fires in the house.

Mrs Bruce-Cole continued to live in Claremont with her children until 1948 when it was sold to the council for £14,000. Henleaze Infant and Junior schools were then built on the adjoining land which included the grass tennis courts used by the family and friends just past the grassy bank on the right of the front drive to Claremont.

Resident Derek Wilding, who attended Claremont Henleaze Infant School in the late 1940s/early 1950s recalls:

> I remember that the caretaker/gardener at Claremont was called Mr Sweeting. He lived somewhere near the old stables (now mews cottages).

> In the early 1950s the partly unmade road up to Claremont was known to me as Coach Drive (now Henleaze Park). The trees in the grounds of St Margaret's High School for Girls (replaced by chalet bungalows in the 1960s) were very tall and produced some interesting noises in high winds.

Claremont then became a local authority school for children with special needs *(see also further information under Schools)*.

Some personal recollections from local resident, Derek Reynolds, in 1990 included:

> Claremont was my Aunt's home as a child until her elopement – more of that later! Mr Caleb Bruce-Cole, my Aunt's father, was the proprietor of the Packer and Carson chocolate business with three factories in Bristol. He died at the age of 49 (1912) and it was reputed that he would have been a millionaire, if he had lived.

> Mrs Bruce-Cole was a very autocratic lady, so it astonished me to hear her grandchildren calling her 'Gaggy'. I remember being invited to dinner – when a schoolboy, on my own – and being treated like royalty! Fetched by the chauffeur wearing his black leather gaitered uniform driving a large Buick; he surprised me by putting a rug on my lap and tucking it around my bare legs.

> Dinner was served in a large mahogany panelled dining room with windows down one side and a bay window at one end. The table could have seated over 20 guests but there were only three of us, Mrs Bruce-Cole, her French companion and myself. It was like a scene from the film *Little Lord Fauntleroy*.

My Mother's family lived nearby in Grange Court Road and it was my uncle, Leslie Huxtable, who married Joyce Bruce-Cole in very romantic circumstances. He, no doubt, was an unacceptable suitor as he would have just been de-mobilised after the First World War from the Gloucestershire regiment and had neither money nor profession, so it had to be a secret runaway marriage. This was achieved by using a ladder placed under Joyce's bedroom window in Claremont House one night and silently stealing away. The marriage was, in fact, a success with a family of two boys and three girls.

Mrs Bruce-Cole continued to live in the house through World War II. Chickens and, I think, a pig were kept on this mini farm then plus a Jersey cow which meant that the family did not suffer too much from the 2oz butter ration! No part of the house or grounds was requisitioned in the war but it became the property of Bristol Council after Mrs Bruce-Cole died in about 1950.

It is distressing to see the external appearance of this fine house so spoilt by the addition of metal fire escapes so inappropriately placed on the front of the building. (*See also further information under Schools.*)

Henley's House (Henleaze Park)

This substantial property built of stone with a slate roof was situated approximately 400 feet above sea level (122 metres) on land now occupied by the Longleat Close and St Margaret's Drive chalet bungalows. It was set in extensive parklands and faced west and south west with fine views of Kingsweston, Blaise Castle and the Welsh Hills. In 1659 the old house and lands were sold for £540 by Ralph Sadleir – grandson of Ralph Sadleir, Henry VIII's courtier – to Robert Henley. It then became known as Henley's House. In 1701 the house appears to have been owned by James Burton.

Henleaze Park

In 1769 the estate was owned by Edward Bright and in 1779 by Phillip Protheroe. In 1815 the Protheroe's, who owned a great deal of property in Westbury, including Cote House and Springfield, sold Henleaze Park to John Savage who ran a sugar refinery in Wilder Street, St Paul's with his

Henleaze Park, *c*1913
The house was built in the 1700s and demolished in the 1960s. Chalet bungalows known as St Margaret's Drive and Longleat Close were then built. (*Mike Brooks collection*)

brother, Francis. John is described as being 'in manner, dress and appearance a capital type of the English gentleman of the old school, courteous, hearty and hospitable'. He married Miss Rachael Claxton and they had a daughter Maria, who died at Henleaze, in 1842, aged 18 years. John Claxton Savage, B.A. Oriel Coll. Oxford, their eldest son died at Oxford in 1836, aged 23 years.

In 1844 John Savage advertised Henleaze Park for sale, with 100 acres (40 hectares). In 1851 the property was described as 'pleasantly situated on the summit of extensive park-like grounds, well stocked with timber trees'.

The house was then owned by Mr William Poole King, a Bristol merchant, who moved to Clifton around 1853. Mr John P. Budgett lived there until 1867 and Mrs Budgett until 1871 when it was sold for £13,400. Later occupiers were Walter Derham who subsequently let it to Samuel Derham, a shoe manufacturer, who died in 1886. Mrs Derham lived there until 1906, and Percival Rogers, of A K Brewery fame, with his wife Kitty until about 1915. Percival and Kitty had three sons, Gerald, Clifford and Hubert. Mrs Rogers, whose family lived in Goldney House, Clifton, was formerly Kitty Fry. The Rogers' herd of Guernsey cows grazed on both sides of the semi-circular drive, lined with beech trees, which led up from the familiar Thatched Cottage Lodge (now 166 Henleaze Road).

In the early 1900s the farm (where the Esso petrol station now stands on Henleaze Road) was let to the George Brothers who lived in 12 The Drive and 166 Henleaze Road (both lodges of Henleaze Park). The kitchen garden was let to Mr Hookings who ran it as a market garden.

Henleaze Park with its estate of 46 acres (18 hectares) was put up for auction at the Grand Hotel, Broad Street, Bristol, in 1913. The reserve price of £10,000 was not reached at the auction, £8,700 being the highest bid.

There were gardens, lawns, an orchard, glasshouses, stabling, two lodges (now 166 Henleaze Road and 12 The Drive) and various farm buildings on the estate.

The house was entered by a handsome stone portico outer hall, with stained glass door, leading to the inner hall, with carved marble and free-stone pillar supports, with a dome-lighted roof and gallery. There was 'commodious cellarage', a well of spring water and pump on the premises, plus water and gas from the mains. On the ground floor there was a morning room with a bay window with an Adams design mantelpiece. The dining room had a similar mantelpiece as well as a tiled grate. The drawing room had a white marble mantelpiece, and there was a spacious library as well as domestic accommodation comprising china pantry, servants' sitting room, butler's pantry, large kitchen with excellent range, scullery with rainwater pump, housekeeper's room, larder, wine cellar, WC and other offices.

There were two staircases, one of stone with a gracefully designed ironwork balustrade leading to the first floor containing eight bed and dressing rooms, night and day nurseries, bathroom and WC. The second floor contained a further four bedrooms and there was a staircase approach to the roof.

The private grounds in 1913 consisted of approximately two acres (one hectare) and contained a stone built pagoda, arbours and summerhouses, an ornamental rockery and pool, a wilderness and fern garden. Shrubs and ornamental trees included Wellingtonias, Palms, Scotch Firs, Oak, Elm, Cedars, Chestnut, Holm Oak and Copper Beech.

There were two stables containing seven stalls and two large loose boxes as well as harness rooms, a spacious yard, other outhouses, dog kennels and a coach house. Accommodation for three motor cars was also provided in 1913! There were two walled-in gardens with a range of glass houses (with hot water boilers), a peach house, vines, apple, pear, cherry and plum trees.

After the auction a group of interested parties comprising F. N. Cowlin, the builders, Wansbrough, the solicitors and Horace Walker, Chairman of

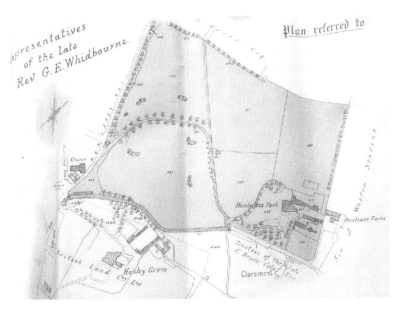

Henleaze Park House – Estate Plan, 1920s
The house became St Margaret's School (1924–1962) (*Bristol Record Office*)

H. J. Packer & Co Ltd (chocolate manufacturers) bought the property for £8,750 and in 1915 some 44 acres (18 hectares) of the park were sold. Wansbrough's were involved in developing part of the land as Wanscow Walk, Henleaze Park Drive and Hill View.

In 1923 Henleaze Park House was sold to Sidney Curtis of Springfield Farm for £20,500. In 1924 he then sold it to Reverend G A K Simpson and his wife Caroline who had been living locally in Downs Park West. They then opened the property as St Margaret's High School for Girls *(see further details in chapter on Schools).* In 1925 part of the remaining land was sold to the builder Monk Bros for £787-10s-0d (£787.50) to build some properties in Henleaze Park Drive.

Henley Park Grove Mansion

This property, said to be an early eighteenth-century farmhouse, was situated between the present Drive and Fallodon Way. The western border was Henleaze Road and the eastern one Park Grove and Springfield Grove. Much of the land had been sold off for new houses from the early 1900s so the grounds were greatly reduced by the time the mansion was demolished in the 1960s.

Thomas Powell lived there from 1825 until 1838 when Samuel Cox succeeded him. In 1843 the sale of the house and furniture was announced as the vendor, Wiltshire Cox was 'about to leave the neighbourhood.' It remained empty until 1851 and was later occupied by Thomas Chope, Mr C.H. Low, Captain William Alcock (1875–79), Colonel Rooke and by Thomas Owen, MP for Launceston who died there in 1898. Young Mr Alcock, who hunted with Lord Fitzhardinge's hounds, used to keep his horses in some sheds on the land where Cavendish Road now stands.

After the death of Thomas Owen, the Owen family, comprising of Elizabeth, Charley Todd and Owen, put the house up for auction at the Bank Auction Mart at Corn Street in June 1898. It was sold to the British Land Company of 25 Moorgate Street, London for £17,000.

The 1898 brochure described it as follows:

The House is set in over 20 acres [eight hectares] of grounds charmingly laid out with lawns, tennis court, flower gardens, two vegetable gardens and an orchard with well stocked selected fruit trees The winding carriage drive is guarded at both front and back entrances by tastefully designed lodges. The forest and ornamental timbers consist of Cedar of Lebanon, Deodara Cedar, Pine, Yew, Limes, Oak, and Sycamore etc. The glass houses include a peach house, 32 feet long [10 metres] and orchard, tomato and rose house 170 feet long [52 metres] and a vine house, 124 ft long [38 metres].

The Stables stand in a spacious yard with three stalls, two loose or foaling boxes, harness room, heated carriage house, and fodder loft. There is also housing nearby for 12 cattle, a calf house, food & boiling houses, and superior piggeries.

Ground floor
This comprises of an entrance hall, morning room, central hall with fireplaces, noble drawing room with french windows, finely proportioned dining room with buffet recess, wine cupboard and three french windows, a lobby with gentlemen's lavatory, butler's pantry, smoking room, large kitchen, pantry, back kitchen, larder, dairy, servants' hall. From the morning room a spacious conservatory with luxuriant palms is reached and then a billiard room with an arched ceiling with good natural lighting for daytime play.

The halls and lobbies have tiled floors and the reception rooms, staircase and halls are heated by radiators.

First floor

There are eight bedchambers, two dressing rooms, bathroom (with photographic developing cupboard) housemaids' closets (with hot and cold water). A back staircase from the servants' apartments on the ground floor leads to this bedroom floor and the servants' bedrooms on the second floor.

The house was derelict and empty for some years in the early 1900s but it was then used as a Ladies College of Domestic Science from 1905 to 1911 and run by Miss Violet Bland. It appears that Sylvia Pankhurst of the suffragette family may have lived there for a short while around 1914. In 1919 approval was granted for the house to be converted into six flats.

Below is a list showing information sources for some of the occupants from 1825 to 1967:

1825	Jury List	Thomas Powell, Merchant
1838	Survey House and 21 acres (eight hectares), rateable value £135.	Owner occupier, Samuel Cox
1841	Census	Occupier, Elliott Roberts, independent
1843	Survey House, offices and park	Occupier, Elliott Roberts Proprietor, Wiltshire Cox
1880	Directory	William Alcock
1885	Directory	Col. Rooke
1895	Directory	Thomas Owen, MP (for Launceston)
1897	Directory	Thomas Owen, MP & Nat. Liberal Club. He died in 1898.
1908/9	Directories	Miss Violet Bland Ladies College of Domestic Science
1919	Approval granted to:	P. J. E. Lockton to convert to six flats
1924	Resident of No.3 flat	Miss G. Hope-Evans (church committee)
1924	Planning Approval	Two cottage flats to be built in Mansion to cost a maximum of £1,000
1950	Directory	The Mansion then had eight occupants

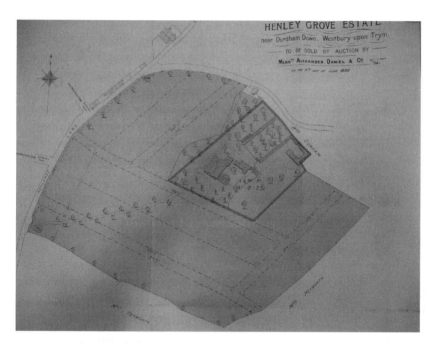

Henley Grove Mansion Estate Plan, 1898
The eighteenth century house was subsequently demolished in the 1960s and the site used for new houses in Lawrence and Henley Groves. (*Bristol Record Office*)

1847-53

Sketch books by Edward Earle (in the Bristol Record Office) depict Henley Grove House.

In 1924 the surrounding area was being developed into large semi-detached houses.

Henley Park Grove Mansion had very large rooms with ornate ceilings and cornices and elegant fireplaces. Along one side where there were long windows there was a very large long room that could have been a ballroom. On the front of the building was the tower room that gave a very good view. There was a large courtyard to the rear of the house with coach houses and stables. Under the house were spacious cellars with storage racks for wine, and a butchery store with slabs for carving and hooks for hanging meat.

The house was left to Mr W. O. Weeks by his father, a builder, who had built many houses in Muller Road, Horfield. He sold it to McGill for £17,000 in 1967. The owners of Owen & Owen, the department store in Bath, were some time linked with the property. Last known residents included Mr Mabey who was connected with the Port of Bristol, a Mr Jenkins, Mr Bysant, and Mr & Mrs Weeks. There were seven flats occupied in all.

In November 1967 the house was demolished for redevelopment of the site into 20 'town houses' which were marketed at £6,500. There were several very old cedar trees which it was hoped would be preserved, but at 7.30am one morning the developers cut one down and would probably have taken more down but council officials were called by nearby residents to prevent further felling. The developer was later fined £500, a small price to pay to enable the sale of 20 houses at £6,500 each. In 1999 one property sold for £135,000.

The Manor House (Southmead Manor)

This house is situated in Southmead Road near the junction with Wellington Hill West. It was first mentioned in 1319 in the Worcester Register of Bishop Cobham who granted to Henry, son of Ralph and Isobel Croke 'licence to hear Divine Service in their Chapel within their Manor House at Southmead in the Parish of Westbury, so long as the rights and customs of the Parish Church are not injured'.

The Manor House became the property of the Nunnery of St Mary Magdalene, which was situated at the bottom of St Michael's Hill. The Nunnery was one of the first to be disbanded in 1539 by Henry VIII. At that time Thomas Haines had been granted a long-term lease on the Manor House by the Prioress. However King Henry subsequently granted the Manor to the Haines family on reversion of the fee.

The Barker family bought the property some years later and remained there until 1676. Then it was sold to John Knight (Lord Mayor in 1690) who had made a fortune in sugar refinery in Bristol. On his death the property was inherited by his son Jacob Knight and subsequently his son Thomas who eventually sold the estate in 1743. The Manor was then bought by a rich linen draper, John Clark, whose widow subsequently sold it to Joshua James in 1785. By 1797 the estate was leased to John Weeks, famous landlord of the Bush Tavern; it was later sold to Thomas Jones, attorney, to meet debts. However some of the creditors objected and the Courts ordered in 1803 that it should be auctioned.

In 1803 Richard Llewellin, owner of a local brewery, purchased Southmead Manor and its estate of 313 acres (127 hectares). It stayed in his family until 1872 when it was purchased by Mr H. W. Green. In 1877 Dr Badock (later Sir Henry) bought the House and on his death in 1892 it was sold to F. Holman. In the 1900s the house was occupied by the Holman family. Some fine walnut trees bordered on to Henleaze Lane then and were very tempting for the village boys. Much of the

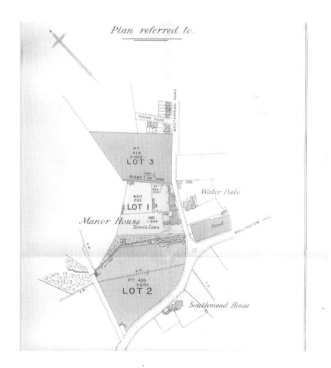

Plan referred to.

Manor House Plan, 1926
Sold off in three lots. Left – Manor House. Right – Waterdale House off Southmead
Road. In the forefront Southmead House which later provided accommodation for the
Blind School pupils. (*Mike Brooks collection*)

original house was destroyed around 1910–12 when it was almost
rebuilt.

When Frank Holman died the estate comprising of over nine acres
(three and a half hectares) was put up for auction in three lots on 15 July,
1926 by Stanley, Alder & Price and Chappell & Matthews, auctioneers at
the Grand Hotel, Bristol.

Lot 1 – More than two acres (one hectare) contained the Manor House
with its nine bedrooms, schoolroom, domestic offices, library, dining and
drawing rooms, heated vinery and conservatory etc. plus outbuildings,
kitchen garden, orchards, woodlands, 70 feet long (21 metres) open air
swimming pool, mature lawns with room for two tennis courts.

Lot 2 – Excellent Paddock forming a valuable and choice building site;
nearly four acres (one and a half hectares), where the 1930 Glenwood
Road properties and the houses bordering Southmead Road to Lake Road
now stand.

Lot 3 – Enclosure of pasture land forming a valuable building site; nearly two and a half acres (one hectare), roughly where Southmead Police Station now stands.

Dr Robert Courtney and his wife, Mary Courtney, moved into the Manor in 1938. Both were Scots and became extremely well-known in the community. Their garden, approximately 2 acres (one hectare) was lovingly tended by a part-time gardener and was opened on many occasions for fêtes and garden parties. It was rumoured that there was a secret passage from the Manor going right through to the Abbey in Abbey Road, Westbury-on-Trym. Dr Courtney thought they would open it up in case the house was demolished in the bombing raids of World War II. The entry was under the stone floor inside the porch, but it proved impenetrable, having been bricked up unknown years before. Dr Courtney died in 1976 and Mrs Courtney in 1986. Marjorie Bath worked as a housekeeper for the Courtney's from 1943–86.

The house was then passed to a niece Jean Greenland who sold it to Mr and Mrs Clive Hughes. The property is currently being run as a nursery school.

The ruin behind 22 Lake Road butts against the walled garden boundary of the Manor. This is now a Grade II listed building whose architectural details indicate that it was built in the late seventeenth or early eighteenth century. It is one of the earliest examples of garden architecture in Bristol.

Springfield House (Northumberland House)

Around 1815 John Protheroe, the owner of Springfield, let the house to Francis Walter Savage who had set up as a sugar refiner in Wilder Street, St Pauls with his brother, John. After a long tenancy Francis bought the house. He married Julia Louisa Walker, from Redland, and they had two sons, Francis and Charles, and a daughter, Frances. Francis Senior died in 1845 and Julia in 1857. Their son Francis then owned the estate and continued to live there with his brother Charles. Francis died in 1891 and Charles inherited and lived until he died in December 1894. His sister, Frances Harriet Heyworth then inherited a life interest and lived there until about 1902. Mr Percy L Hughes-Garbett occupied the house until about 1912 when Miss Percy moved in.

Hugh Conway (Frederick John Fargus), born in Bristol in 1847, enjoyed considerable international fame as a novelist. His book *A Family Affair* is about Beatrice who has two uncles, Horace and Herbert Talbert, who live in Hazlewood House, Oakbury. The author based the characters of the uncles on Francis and Charles Savage and the house on Springfield. The novel gives an excellent insight into the routine of life in a large Henleaze house in the 1800s, like securing the house each night by closing and bolting the shutters and putting the silver away in chamois bags in a safe.

Northumberland House

The name of Springfield House was changed to Northumberland House whilst occupied by Col. Heyworth-Savage. It was still in his possession in March 1916 when solicitor Jeremiah Osborne swore a statutory declaration to confirm his title. It is assumed that there were no formal deeds of the property extant at that time. The declaration was necessary to enable him to convey part of the estate – 11 acres (four and a half hectares) to the east side of Henleaze Road – to H. H. Wills, who simultaneously conveyed a portion, approximately two acres (one hectare) behind the houses in Howard Road, to Clifton High School for Girls.

Northumberland House. Porch & Side of House.

Northumberland House, c1915
An imposing mansion built around 1820 was set among formal rose gardens; remnants of the marble and parquet floors survived long after the building was demolished. (*M J Tozer collection*)

When Miss Percy, from the well-known Northumberland family, moved into Northumberland House around 1912 it became known as Northumberland House School *(see further details in chapter on Schools).*

Waterdale House

The original house, demolished in the late 1800s, had been a working farm. It was on the site of the present fire station in Southmead Road.

The new house, originally owned by an American, boasted a range of model piggeries in the paddock. During World War II some of the tiles from the roof of the piggeries were used to replace ones broken during the 1940s air raids. The pantry was on the north east side of the house and had been there when it was a farmhouse. The floors and shelves were all made of Welsh slate. Cold food to be cooked the next day had to be brought into the kitchen the night before to unfreeze. It was possible to peer over the encircling high wall and see the lake and its small rowing boat amid the rushes. Boating there was one of the Sunday School treats organised by the Southmead Mission. The nearby stream in Wellington Hill West was culverted in the early 1900s.

During the 1930s the grounds were open once a year for the outing of the Sunday School children from Westbury-on-Trym church who used to all walk there. They were able to enjoy the rural setting and the lake.

Waterdale House, June 1959
Taken at 7am. Demolished in the 1960s and replaced by Waterdale Close and Gardens, off Wellington Hill West. (*Griffey family collection*)

The Griffey family were the last occupants. In 1990 Natalie recalled: 'There were nine bedrooms and three large reception rooms. In the gardens stood a shepherd's cottage that contained a miniature Adam fireplace in which a fire was lit to warm the ice skaters on the lake in winter.' Waterdale was demolished in the mid-1960s to make way for the present Waterdale Close houses.

Westmead House (The Monastery)

These premises are situated in Brecon Road. It appears that Sir Edward Protheroe, a local merchant, had Westmead built for his mother who unfortunately died before its completion.

Westmead House

The house was then sold to Mr Irving, a Methodist minister, and then to the Visitation Order of enclosed nuns in 1831. The 1841 Tithe Map shows this property as Westmead House.

The Monastery

The number of nuns increased and the community was determined to build a proper monastery on site. Building started on the main buildings in 1859 and was completed in 1862. The 1881 ordnance survey map show the name change to the Monastery.

In the 1890s the Visitation Order invited the Sisters of Mercy, then living in Dighton Street, to take tea at the Convent, by a happy coincidence on the Feast of St Ursula's. Tea was evidently also a pleasant occasion as the Sisters of Mercy bought the Convent in 1896 (on the occasion of the Golden Jubilee of their arrival in Bristol) to use as a boarding school. The Convent and its 10 acres (four hectares) of land were purchased for £9,000 on the 21st July 1896.

In 1897 it was opened as a boarding school for girls under the patronage of Saint Ursula (see further details in chapter on Schools).

PART 3
LODGE HOUSES

Claremont Lodge and Cottage

The Lodge and Cottage were the homes of the chauffeur and the gardener. Claremont Lodge was renovated and extended in the 1980s and fronts Henleaze Park.

Claremont Court

The stables were converted into mews cottages and the single part of Claremont Cottage was demolished to complete the new development Claremont Court. On one of the flagstones in the courtyard is the date 1897 and there is a milestone marker embedded into the wall bearing the initials W.P. showing the Westbury Parish boundary in 1897.

Henleaze Park Lodges
166 Henleaze Road

This is one of two former Henleaze Park Lodges and must surely be the most photographed home in the area due to its attractive thatched roof, tiny gothic windows and age – circa 1810 – dated by the original reed thatch which was considered to be much stronger than straw. Similar cottages, designed by John Nash and built around 1811, can be seen at Blaise Hamlet. It has never been verified that Nash also built this property.

The lodge's most unusual feature is the spy window on the ground floor that allowed the coach from Henleaze Park House to be seen from either the sitting or dining rooms.

Early 1900s

Rose Clery (née George) wrote in 1992 that her father and Uncle Harry (who lived in this thatched cottage) rented the farm and field of Henleaze Park and ran it as Henleaze Park Dairy until 1921. (The 1906 Samuel Loxton sketch of the then Henleaze Congregational Church clearly shows the farmyard wall the other side of Henleaze Road.)

Henleaze Park Lodges
166 Henleaze Road 1994: Craftsmen at work on the new thatched roof in September.
(*Sylvia Kelly collection*)

The kitchen/living room of the lodge was papered in plain red. On the walls hung a set of humorous hunting prints, the red coats of the hunting characters matching the walls behind. The sitting room always seemed to be full of potted ferns and there was a pond close by where watercress grew.

1913

The main entrance to Henleaze Park was here and one of the last carriages to use this front drive may have been that of Mrs Fry of Goldney House (Chocolates and Quakerism) whose daughter was married to Percy Rogers. She was driven over from Clifton in a carriage and pair to visit her family.

1958

The thatched roof that had not been attended to for over 100 years was renewed by its owner, Helen McLachlan in 1958. Webbers of Dunster, in Somerset, a thatching family for some 400 years, undertook the re-thatch.

1972

A beautiful fir tree in the garden became diseased and had to be removed.

1977

The Department of the Environment listed the property for its historical interest and special architecture.

1995

Mrs Elise Beauchamp won a Bristol Civic Society Environmental Award, one of only ten in the city, for the beautiful new thatch. This was renewed in 1994 by a Wiltshire firm in the traditional nineteenth-century way.

12 The Drive

This Grade II listed building former Henleaze Park Lodge is located opposite St Peter's Church.

After the publication of the first edition of *The Henleaze Book*, Rosa Clery sent the following fascinating information on her childhood home in the early 1900s:

> My father, Edwin George was born in the 1880s in one of the cottages 177–205 Henleaze Road, now demolished.
>
> The picture shows 12 The Drive as it was about 1912. The nearest house was 'Granny Young's' cottage at the bottom of The Drive, now 132 Henleaze Road. [This was one of the lodges to the Henley Grove estate.]
>
> My sister and I are standing just inside the field called 'The Park', which lay between us and the 'Front Drive' [leading up to Henleaze Park House from the other lodge, the thatched cottage on Henleaze Road].
>
> A fine row of elms ran across the Park [see 1903 Ordnance survey map].
>
> There was a large white gate that could be shut across the road: a similar one was outside my uncle's house – the thatched lodge – dating from the time when both houses were lodges to Henleaze Park. In my father's boyhood the 'big house' was occupied by Mr Walter

Henleaze Park Lodge
12 The Drive, c1912: Rosa George was born in 1905 and her sister Winifred in 1906. They are standing just inside the field called The Park that lay between The Drive and Wanscow Walk. (*George family collection*)

Derham who owned the whole estate. In my childhood it was occupied by the family of Mr Percy Rogers – I remember being taken there to 'nursery tea'.

Our house had four downstairs rooms. The front ones opened on each side of the heavy wooden front door. One was special – only used on Sundays and special occasions. The other was the kitchen/living room, the centre of everything. It had a stone flagged floor covered with linoleum and mats and rugs. The wallpaper was varnished with a design of red poppies on a cream background. On one side of the room was a range for cooking, hot water and general comfort. A kettle or saucepan always seemed to be simmering on the back of the stove. Above the range was a high mantle shelf on which stood a brass candlestick and above that a fine overmantle in oak carved by my father.

On one side of the range was my mother's low chair and on the other my father's Windsor armchair. The room also contained a horsehair sofa and a fine settle made and carved by my father. This and the old grandfather clock subsequently went to my brother's house in Westbury-on-Trym.

Behind this living room was a room that for some reason we called the 'pantry'. One wall was filled with built-in shelves and cupboards. It had a deep low windowsill on which we kept wildflower collections, boxes of caterpillars and silkworms, jars of tadpoles and other treasures of a country childhood. This room also contained a small bookcase and table for the ledgers of the farm finance.

This room led into the 'back kitchen', stone flagged and whitewashed containing the sink with one coldwater tap. The draining 'board' was a slab of smooth slate. In one corner was a built-in boiler under which a fire was lit every Monday morning for the weekly wash.

Outside the back door there was a large tank which collected rainwater from the roof. The tank had a tap into the back kitchen and the soft water was used for hair washing. At the back of the house was a disused pump, cages for our rabbits and fantail pigeons, the outside toilet (no indoor sanitation), the coal shed, a rubbish dump; the contents of the latter were collected weekly by the horse-drawn corporation dustcart.

The flower gardens were on each side of the house – on one side rose beds and paths and on the other a lawn and border. There were two laburnum trees, peonies, cornflowers, violets and a passionflower.

Over the front of the house was a magnificent honeysuckle. Just inside the front gate were two rustic seats and my sister and I used to sit on the arm of 'our' seat, clutching the railings and waiting to be greeted by the very occasional passer-by.

There were only two bedrooms. Pillows and mattresses were filled with 'home-grown' feathers and down. A door shut off the staircase in the daytime.

Of course no gas or electricity: oil lamps and candles with nightlights in the bedrooms.

Once a week, the oil-man (by name Mr Downs) came with his horse and cart. The back of the cart opened to reveal a large tank of paraffin with a tap from which our domestic cans were filled.

An essential job every morning was to 'do' the lamps – that is to wash the glass globes and chimney, trim the wicks and refill with paraffin.

The overhang must have made the front rooms rather dark, but I don't remember them being so: it certainly provided a dry place for us to play in even on wet days.

Separate title for 12 The Drive was acquired in 1924 when the front entrance was moved to the west side and the overall size increased by about a third on the east side. An extension doubled the chimney stack and provided a new lounge and a bedroom above, and possibly the whole rear of the house was rearranged to make space for the bathroom and lavatory. The dining room now had two windows, a double and a single – the latter probably being the original front door. There is a stretch of short floorboards in the bedroom above indicating that a stair ran through.

In 1927 the house was purchased by Miss Florence Jane Morse of Clifton for £1,325. Miss Morse died in 1956.

In the 1960s and 70s the property was occupied by Peter Brown, local television journalist, and his family. Heather Brown, his wife, was one of the local residents who launched a forum for discussion in the early 1970s that resulted in the formation of Henleaze Neighbourhood Society. The main entrance has been moved around to the side.

Joe and Cynthia Thornton moved to 12 The Drive in January 1975 from Henleaze Avenue. The original garden was much larger and some land on either side was sold off and houses built. There is a mound in the bottom corner covered with flowers and greenery which has an indestructible concrete air raid shelter below.

In the 1980s a kitchen extension to the left was further extended lengthways and the back door was moved around to the right hand side instead of leading straight on to the garden.

Henley Grove Lodges

84 Henleaze Road

The main lodge for Henley Grove, as the 1841 Tithe Map shows, is located opposite Henleaze Avenue junction. It was still used as the entrance to Henley Grove Mansion until Holmes Grove and Henley Grove were constructed. In 1898 R Bryne, who was responsible for the pasture land and farm buildings of Henley Grove Mansion, lived here. In the early 1900s it was occupied by the sister of Mrs Bruce-Cole and her husband.

132 Henleaze Road

Built in 1844 this property, located by The Drive junction, is now known as Grove Lodge. The black and white timbering of the gable end of the lodge can be seen from the St Peter's Hospice Charity shop across Henleaze Road. It appears to have had only a small footpath to Henley

Henley Grove Lodges
84 Henleaze Road, 2006: Situated on the right of the Henleaze Conservation area. It
was the main lodge for Henley Grove Mansion and is located opposite Henleaze
Avenue junction. (*Bowerman collection*)

Henley Grove Lodges
132 Henleaze Road, c1910: The lodge is on the right with black and white timbering
of the gable end. Although so called it had no route to Henley Grove Mansion until
the 1920s. (*M J Tozer collection*)

Grove Mansion – *see 1903 Ordnance survey map.* (Lawrence Grove was not built until the 1920s.)

Tom Graveney, who played cricket for Gloucestershire and was one of England's finest batsman, lived here for five years after marrying Jackie Brookman, a Henleaze resident, in 1952. They moved to Winchcombe after Jackie's father died in 1957. Tom Graveney was Wisden Cricketer of the Year in 1953.

The property was used as the Polish Consulate from 2003 to 2005.

Springfield House Lodge and Cottages

18 Henleaze Road

Springfield House Lodge, located near the Downs Park East junction, is an attractive historical property, richly decorated in Tudoresque style with gabled windows of Tudor and Italian mix. Its present owners, Mr and Mrs Payne, found a date of 1727 in the building, which appears to make it the oldest inhabited property in Henleaze.

The 1841 Census shows that occupants at that time were Thomas Badman, gardener, 30, Harriet Badman, wife, 30, Samuel, son aged 6,

Springfield Lodge
18 Henleaze Road: Built in 1727. It was the former home of the gardeners of Springfield House. (*Bristol Record Office*)

William, son aged 4, and Ann, daughter aged 2. The 1881 Census lists the gardener, Charles Edwards aged 42 born in Surrey, living there with his wife, Kerusal, aged 38 and their daughter Ellen aged 11.

The lodge became a private property on 4 October 1937 when the Northumberland House estate was sold and broken up. It was owned by the American singer, Diane Solomon, during the 1970s.

Springfield Cottages

31 and 33 Russell Grove, near the tennis courts, are believed to be part of the Springfield estate. There is a well in the garden of 33 that is now covered in.

The 1881 Census lists the following occupants: John Clark, gardener, Head of House, aged 58, Lydia Clark, Lodging Housekeeper, aged 59, Joseph Davis, nephew, footman, aged 26 and Harriet Hort, servant, aged 21.

we GIVE you more

The UK's most visited estate agency website*

YOUR MOVE.co.uk

Online partnerships with leading portals

rightmove.co.uk   propertyfinder.com

fish4homes   *Source: Hitwise March 06

we GET you more

- Interest from serious enquirers
- Best market price
- Viewings from 'matched' buyers
- A quicker sale

IF YOU ARE LOOKING TO SELL YOUR PROPERTY CONTACT **YOUR MOVE** TO SEE HOW YOU CAN 'GET MORE'

YOUR MOVE
OLIVER SCARLETT

Your Move Olive Scarlett
100 Henleaze Road
BRISTOL BS9 4JZ
Tel: 0117 962 9293

PART 4
SCHOOLS

Introduction

Prior to 1952, when the Henleaze Infant and Junior Schools were built in the grounds of the Claremont estate, the majority of younger children attended Cranford House, Henleaze Kindergarten, Horfield School, Park School, Springfield Kindergarten, St Margaret's, Westbury Church of England or Westbury Park schools.

Claremont Henleaze Infant School

In 2006 Derek Wilding, who still lives in the area, was able to supply background information on the start of state primary education in Henleaze:

I was born in July 1944 when my parents were living in Hill View and I attended Claremont Henleaze Infant School from August 1949 to July 1952. My younger sister, Veronica was only there from January 1952.

We do not believe that there was a Claremont Henleaze Junior School but we both remember watching both Henleaze Infant and Henleaze Junior Schools being built.

The Sports Days at Claremont (and early ones at Henleaze possibly) were organised by the Parent Teacher Association and in the early days reflected the problems associated with food rationing – the 'eggs' for the egg and spoon race were billiard balls! I do remember that milk for the Claremont Sports Days was delivered in small churns by Peppard's Dairy in Ashley Down and I was encouraged to collect discarded 'pop' bottles to reclaim the one old penny (less than half a current penny) deposit. I still have a copy of the 'Annual Sports Day' Programme for Saturday 22 July, 1950 with my name in it to prove it.

This afternoon I discovered a class photo for Henleaze Junior School from 1952 or 1953. Apart from me I managed to identify only two or three pupils but I did recognise the Headmaster, Mr Charles. To complete the historical continuity, all three of our children attended Henleaze Infant and Junior Schools.

Claremont School, 1990
The school is in Henleaze Park and is still decorated with lacy woodwork, and enjoying spectacular views over Henleaze. (*Sylvia Kelly collection*)

Claremont School

Claremont House became a school for children with special needs under the local authority in the 1950s. Beryl Corner, a well-known local paediatrician, working with the School Medical Service in the late 1940s and early 1950s helped Claremont School gain a place in history as the first special nursery day school for children with physical impairments to be set up in England. Physiotherapy, movement training and speech therapy are also provided at the school.

Two films were made in the late 1950s and early 1960s – a copy of each is held at the Record Office, Bristol:

Claremont – Children suffering from cerebral palsy are educated and treated at Bristol Education Committee's special school at Claremont. This film won a major Canadian television award and received coast-to-coast showing. It also won a number of British amateur film awards in 1959. Colour/sound, running time –12 minutes.

Back to Claremont – This 1962 film shows the progress made by some of the children featured in *Claremont* (1959). Therapy and teaching, if begun early enough, can produce improvements but sudden and dramatic cures can rarely be achieved. Colour/sound, running time −11 minutes.

In 1963 the annexe was built at the same time as the adjacent chalet bungalows on the former St Margaret's School site.

In 1991 pupils from the school went horse riding at Winford Hospital and Avon Riding Centre for the Disabled at Henbury. The latter is a purpose-built riding school with its own ponies and funds had to be found to subsidise the cost of children riding there. The outings to Henbury took place each Thursday morning. There were 12 spaces that could have been filled several times over. Some of the children were in wheelchairs, but some were able to walk independently. They were fitted with riding hats and cared for by a group of hard working volunteer helpers. Riding at Winford was dependent upon the goodwill of the people who brought their own ponies along to be used so no costs were incurred. For these children riding is a positive activity and it was hoped that other children in the school would continue to have the opportunity to learn to ride.

A new hydrotherapy pool was opened on 23 November 2001.

In 2005 there was an Ofsted inspection; the subsequent report rated Claremont School as 'outstanding.'

Cranford House School

It appears that this school, which closed in the 1920s, was located in Westbury Road. The headmistress was Miss Palmer who subsequently moved to 37 Henley Grove when she retired.

Downs Park School

Between 1911 and 1918 this school, located at 51 Downs Park West was attended by Edyth Edbrooke, author of *Time There Was*, whose autobiography was published under the name of Anne Edbrooke. The school was run by Mrs Kate Milani, BA. Mr Milani was a German violinist with an Italian name. Unfortunately First World War anti-German feelings caused the closure of what had been an excellent school.

Henleaze Infant School

Claremont had several tennis courts just past the sunny bank on the right of the front entrance which were demolished when Henleaze Infant School was built on them in the 1950s. The school opened in 1952.

An informal picnic was held under the chestnut tree in the grounds on Wednesday, 13 July 1977 to commemorate Queen Elizabeth's Silver Jubilee; Henleaze grandparents, parents, children and friends – nearly 100 in total – attended and Bristol International Folk Dancers demonstrated their skills in a colourful way. The Infant School also celebrated its 25th birthday in 1977. An interesting collection of school events, newspapers and trivia was on view, including a ration book from 1952.

On Sunday 2 June 2002, the residents of Henleaze, their friends and relatives celebrated the Queen's Golden Jubilee at the Infant School. Hundreds, young and old, took part in this get-together and participated in the fun activities; many families took picnics and there was a burger barbeque on hand for the hungry.

Henleaze Junior School

In the 1920s Claremont had a herd of six Jersey cows which used to graze on their field adjacent to Springfield Grove, now the site of Henleaze Junior School. Henleaze Junior School opened in 1952.

At the end of her last term in July 1958 Sue Headlam collected autographs from the teachers, including the following who many readers may remember: D. Scannell, R. Crumpton, R. P. Horton, C. M. Riley, J. Burgess, L. R. Charles, P. Barnes, A. Hunter, D. Derrick and J. Lodowska.

On 15 May 1989, the Princess Royal visited the school to receive a cheque for nearly £10,000 for the Save the Children Fund. This money had been raised by 150 schools from all over Avon by various maths activities including a Copper Trail. Almost one million coins had to be paid into the bank in numerous carrier bags before Princess Anne could receive the cheque! Two children and one teacher from each of the 150 participating schools attended the visit, including Henleaze Infant and Claremont. Local children lined the drive to welcome the Princess and other visitors, including the Lord Mayor, the Chairman of Avon County Council and the Director of Education.

Henleaze Kindergarten School

Operated from 106 Henleaze Road – above the Cavendish Hairdressing Salon – from 1935–37. These premises are now occupied by Parkhouse, the Solicitors.

Miss Rutter's

This small kindergarten school was run by the Misses Edith and Mabel Rutter from their home at 32 Henleaze Gardens during the 1930s and 1940s. They had a maximum of eight pupils at any one time. There was no plaque outside the house indicating that there was a school in part of the building.

Northumberland House School

When Miss Percy, from the well-known Northumberland family, moved into Northumberland House around 1912 it then became known as

Northumberland House School Production, *c*1934
Joan Sanderson starred in *The Rivals*, (Sheridan) (*Bristol Record Office*)

Northumberland House School. On her death Mr Maw bought the school and his wife became headmistress until the mid-1930s. The school operated there for about 25 years.

During the First World War (1914–18) part of the grounds were taken over as allotments – see 1930 aerial view of Henleaze.

One of the girls, Deborah Kerr-Trimmer, appeared in a school production of *The Mad Hatter's Tea Party*. Under her stage name Deborah Kerr she went on to achieve world-wide recognition and acclaim in the 1950s, appearing as the governess in *The King and I*, with Yul Brynner. Joan Sanderson, a well-known actress, who starred with Peggy Ann Wood in *After Henry* and appeared in numerous television productions, taught elocution at the school. She was also in the school production of *The Rivals* (Sheridan) c1934.

In 1937 the house was sold and demolished. The relics were sent to Mrs Carrington, wife of Murray Carrington, the actor and a member of the Hughes-Garbett family.

When interviewed in 1985 by Carole Gough, Molly, a local resident, recalled the school being pulled down. The local children found several wells and cellars full of racks where wine had been stored. The land was dug up for drainage and the concrete roads were laid in readiness for a garden estate of semis and detached properties. All building stopped during World War II and the land was sold off as allotments, which were quickly snapped up in the 'grow food for victory' era. After the war, prefabs were built on the site. (*See Part 9 – section on Prefabs*)

Park School

67 Park Grove, formerly the home of Park School, is near the junction of Park Grove and Henleaze Park Drive. In November 1926 approval for the use of this new property as a private school was granted. The principals and owners from 1927 were Gordon Sangster Rivington, BA and Miss Cara Thwaites.

Mr Rivington graduated from Hertford College, Oxford University. In the First World War he had served as a Captain in the Sherwood Foresters and had suffered trench fever and shrapnel wounds. He was a great sportsman and particularly enjoyed hockey and tennis; he had won an Oxford 'Blue' in hockey and was captain at a local tennis club in Grange Court Road (now the gardens of Grange Court flats). His three sons Peter, John and Gervase Rivington all attended Park School.

In 1935 Park School is listed as a day school for boys and a member of the Association of Preparatory Schools. The age range was from five to 14 years, the number of pupils averaged 35–40 and there were four or five full time and two part-time staff. The Rev Langley Webb, vicar of St Peter's Church taught scripture at the school. Mrs Kathleen Rivington accompanied singing – on the piano – and supervised painting and drawing for the little ones.

Cooked lunches were served each day; the annual highlight was the Shrove Tuesday pancakes. The annual school outing was by charabanc to Burnham-on-Sea where the boys enjoyed rides on the donkeys and sand digging. Pupils sat the Common Entrance Examination for schools that included Clifton College, Dover College, Blundells, Kelly College and Bryanston.

The boys wore pink caps and ties. Sports included cricket, football, swimming, PE and outdoor races against other schools. There were many school matches and opponents included Clifton College Preparatory, Avondale, XIV, Braidlea and Colchester House.

Mr Rivington died in 1939 and the property was sold to Harold Robinson, a schoolmaster from Clifton. It appears that the school closed down during World War II, probably due to the heavy bombing in Bristol, and became a private residence in 1945.

Red Maids' School

Red Maids' school was established in 1634 and is now the oldest surviving girls' school in England. Jean Vanes, author of *Apparelled in Red: The History of Red Maids' School* wrote:

Miss Marion Webb became Headmistress of Red Maids' School in 1906 with a salary of £200 per annum, a residence in school and a pension fund arrangement. The School at Burfield House, previously owned by Sir Robert Symes, was largely her creation. After extensive alterations the move from Denmark Street took place during the summer holidays of 1911. (Burfield now contains the administrative offices of Red Maids' School.)

In 1911 the girls thought Burfield, situated off Westbury Road, beautiful and were impressed by its rural surroundings. The school fields had been temporarily let to a farmer, so sheep and cattle grazed there. Westbury-on-Trym was a small country village and a wicket gate opened to fields where the houses in Falcondale Road now stand. The grounds of the School were extensive. The drive was lined with trees and there was a lily pond outside the study window.

There were four dormitories instead of two and each girl had her own cubicle with a curtain that could be drawn across for privacy. The four bathrooms on each floor were also welcomed, after those in Denmark Street, which were all in the basement.

In July 1916, overwhelmed by the appalling stream of casualties from the Somme, the Red Cross asked for the use of the building as a hospital. Two hundred beds were proposed and the Red Cross agreed to meet all the costs of the School's temporary move to Manor Place, Clifton, plus re-instatement for the Westbury premises at the end of the War. The girls were not able to return to Burfield until after the beginning of 1920 because of the extensive repairs and redecoration that were necessary.

In the early 1930s a new classroom block was built in the grounds, and further buildings were added in the 1970s.

In the early 1940s provision was made for the oncoming air-raids by reinforcing the cellars to provide accommodation for the younger boarders and two air raid shelters in the grounds (one of which still survives) for the use of staff and sixth form. In September 1940, during the daylight air raids on Filton, many windows were broken and the door of one of the outside shelters was damaged. Staff took turns to act as ARP wardens and firewatchers during the nights and the girls made balaclavas, seaboot stockings and socks for the Armed Forces. There are lively accounts of staff 'kicking' incendiary bombs from the roof of the main building and the caretaker dousing them with sand. In recent years the school has taken great trouble to record the account of girls who were there during World War II and provide them as a 'living history' resource for local primary schools.

In 2003 the school underwent its most significant change when it ended boarding and become a day-school. This decision enabled the Headmistress and Board of Governors to focus once again on fulfilling the original intentions of its founder, John Whitson, by providing education for Bristol women. 2004/05 saw huge investment in the site with the building of a floodlit all-weather sports surface, a complete refurbishment of the 1970s Whitson Sixth Form Centre and major investment in the Music Department and School Library.

The Royal School For The Blind

The Bristol Royal School and Workshops for the Blind was instituted in 1793 and incorporated in 1832. The school was formerly situated at the top of Park Street where Bristol University now stands.

When a revision to the 1832 Act of Parliament came into force in 1905 the Committee of the Bristol Royal School and Workshops for the Blind was able to sell the institution at the top of Park Street and to buy land and build a School for the Blind. The land purchased was approximately 11 acres (four and a half hectares) and was bounded by Henleaze Road, Southmead Road and two lanes now known as Hill View and Oakwood Road. The area was mostly pasture land but also included a large house known as Southmead House. The house had large kitchen gardens with appropriate outbuildings, stables, garages, greenhouses, lawns and flower beds.

Building started in 1907 and the purpose-built school was given the above name by King George V in 1911 when it opened in Henleaze. In 1930 the School had 85 elementary and 22 technical pupils. The School had its own Scout Troop and their neckerchiefs were dark blue. Their flag bore the inscription '227th Bristol (St Peter's Henleaze) with the R.S.B.'

In 1949 a full-length outdoor swimming pool was installed for pupils, but, after a short time, local children were invited in at 'off-peak' times for a nominal fee. It became a popular venue in the summer for local mothers and their children. However in 1971 it was filled in with earth and debris when the new development of neo-Georgian houses/estate started but its outline can still be clearly seen on the open space left.

The Free French Airforce occupied the school during World War II. They trained at Filton on aircraft engines.

The schoolchildren were evacuated to Templecombe, Somerset from 1941–45. The original students were boarders and came from as far afield as Cornwall, Hampshire, Devon and Dorset as well as Gloucestershire, Somerset and Wiltshire and ranged in age from 5 to 16 years. Between 1947 and 1953 there was a big increase in the numbers of pupils at the school, due to a 'new' type of blindness caused through an eye condition known as retrolental-fibroplasia. When medical science found the cause of this disease, the cure rapidly followed.

In later years, weekly boarders and day pupils were taken from local areas and at the school's peak there were 126 pupils on the school roll. However, by 1964, the numbers had decreased mainly through a decline in babies being born, or becoming, blind in early infancy as well as a

Royal School for the Blind, *c*1920
This was a purpose-built boarding school for visually handicapped children from the
south west. (*M J Tozer collection*)

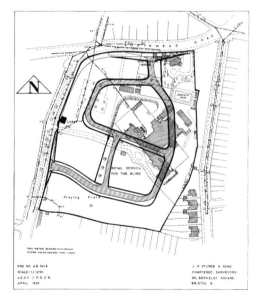

Blind School site plan, 1969
The Bristol Royal School and Workshops for the Blind and land of approximately 11
acres were sold by public auction in 1970. The approved road scheme at that time has
been superimposed. (*Mike Brooks collection*)

change in educational and vocational training policies for blind students from 16 years of age.

The school had many social events over the years including garden fêtes, craftwork exhibitions, plays, choral concerts, prize-giving ceremonies, sports days and flower shows. The programme for the 1953 Coronation celebrations showed the school as the venue for the Henleaze and District Flower Show on 11 July.

The school was Church of England and attached to St Peter's, Henleaze. Sunday services in the school chapel were open to the public. Singing was led by the school choir accompanied by the organ donated by the Wills family. Mr E.H. Getliff was the headmaster during the latter years of the school's existence.

The freehold land of approximately 11 acres (four and a half hectares), with planning permission, was put on sale by public auction on 28 July 1970 by JP Sturge & Sons at The Grand Hotel, Bristol.

The school was demolished in 1971 and the site was then prepared for 90 neo-Georgian houses. It is still possible to locate the line of the former drive leading up to the school by the pine trees which remain.

Southmead House

The house was situated between the present Southmead Road and Hill View, opposite Lake Road. It had fine lawns and cedar trees and was demolished at the same time as the Royal School for the Blind. Tree preservation orders were placed on several of the mature trees.

It is believed that the house was once the official residence of the Chief of the Bristol Constabulary. Later part of the house was used as an area office for Toc H.

Southmead House became an annexe to the Blind School where the senior boys slept. Some technical training was given there for 16–20 year olds who were taught basketry, chair-caning, machine knitting and piano tuning.

The Lodge

A small well-built lodge stood on Henleaze Road, roughly opposite the present double gates to Old Quarry Park – *see also the 1969 site plan.*

The lodge was occupied by one of the several gardeners and his family. Part of the ground floor was a shop, run by the gardener's wife, where 'school-produced' baskets of many sizes and shapes as well as other items were displayed for sale.

The team of gardeners that worked in the extensive gardens and greenhouses around the school ensured its self-sufficiency as far as garden produce was concerned.

In 1970, when the Blind School site was auctioned, part of the lodge was listed as a lock-up shop, subject to a business tenancy, to Mrs G. M. Saunders at a rent of £200 per annum. A notice to quit was then served to the caretaker who was on a service tenancy and who occupied the remainder of the lodge.

Sacred Heart Convent

The Convent had extensive grounds including a drive to Westbury Road with big gates and fields where Carmarthen Road and surrounding roads now stand. In 1897 it took in 14 girls as boarders under the patronage of Saint Ursula. These boarders first went to St Joseph's School in Waterford Road and then to the parish school of the Franciscans off Kings Drive, Bishopston – about one mile away – to which they could walk through fields and over stiles. Two sisters who taught there carried storm lanterns in winter to guide them.

A decision to discontinue boarding was taken in 1924. The number of girls wanting to attend the day school at the Convent had also grown so

Sacred Heart Convent, *c*1910 (now St Ursula's High School)
View from Carmarthen Road. The wooden crosses are still in place on almost every roof. (*The Sisters of Mercy collection*)

The Convent Public Laundry
The Sisters of Mercy took in washing (from St. Mary's and elsewhere) which was laundered using the modern mechanical aids shown here. (*The Sisters of Mercy collection*)

three new classrooms and a cloakroom were added in 1925 at a cost of £2,087.

St Joseph's School

St Joseph's School operated on the site of the present Leonard Hall, Waterford Road until the early 1900s. The boarders from the Sacred Heart Convent in Brecon Road first went to St Joseph's School from 1897. A school is shown on this site on the first ordnance survey map of the area dated 1881.

St Margaret's School

Henleaze Park House, with the remaining land, was sold in 1915 and renamed St Margaret's High School for Girls. The Reverend G. A. K. Simpson and his wife Caroline bought the school which opened with seven girls. It was subsequently run under the joint headship of Miss Emily

Campbell and her widowed sister, Mrs C. Simpson, from 1924 to 1962. In 1923 the area where Park Grove, Hill View, Oakwood Road etc. are now located was sold off for house building. The school grounds were then 6.25 acres (two and a half hectares), the building had 40 rooms and there were 17 staff.

According to an old school brochure the school was situated in the healthiest part of Clifton – 400 feet (122 metres) above sea level.

Fees per term:
Boarders
under 12 year-olds – 25 guineas (£26.25)
12-18 year-olds – 30 guineas (£31.50)
Day pupils
under 8 years old – 4 guineas (£4.20)
8-14 years old – 5 guineas (£5.25)
14-18 years old – 6 guineas (£6.30)
Stationery and use of books – 7/6d (37p)
Sports included croquet, cricket and lacrosse – 5 shillings (25p)

Netball and hockey were considered quite dangerous in the 1930s. Hockey was subsequently played in the 1950s and 1960s on the YMCA pitch near Phoenix Hedge and tennis on the courts later demolished for part of Ridgehill.

School uniform:
Summer
The cherry red and white dresses were originally checked and then changed to striped with a white collar, panama hat with a band in the school colours, cherry blazer with a badge on the pocket showing the marguerite logo of St Margaret's School, white ankle socks and brown shoes.
Winter
Tan raincoat, brown wool winter coat, dark brown velour hat with a red and white band and a bobble, fawn socks and brown shoes, a tan box pleated gymslip, a plaited brown, white and red girdle, a red and cream tie and a cream blouse; for gym, brown baggy shorts and brown gym knickers with a pocket. The uniform was later updated and included a brown pinafore with its own belt, a gabardine raincoat, a red and white striped scarf, a fawn cardigan with a red stripe.

In World War II the school appears to have been used by a unit of the ATS or the Nursing Yeomanry who were attached to an army blood transfusion unit at Southmead Hospital. They were equipped with large American ambulances and staff cars which were painted a uniform grey with the union jack and the stars and stripes displayed on the doors. The girls moved temporarily to 1 The Crescent, on the junction with Hill View.

The school was Anglican and in the 1950s and 1960s the Ten Commandments were always recited each morning during assembly. The girls were required to stand and wait for the teachers to join them and there would always be one girl who would faint daily. The girls attended St Peter's Church on the annual Founder's Day all wearing a marguerite. The school motto was *Sapiens marguerite*.

The senior teacher was Miss Jenner. Miss John, who was Welsh, was the Head of the boarders and was reputed to be as formidable as her alsatian dog, Nicky. The school had 250 girls at his peak, but by the time it closed on 19 July 1962 the numbers had diminished to 100 day girls and boarders.

The school was demolished in 1963 to make way for the chalet bungalows built by Venn's in St Margaret's Drive and Longleat Close. Some of the boundary walls of the original estate are visible – see 11 and 13 The Drive opposite the old Lodge – now known as Greystone Cottage. Another section is the boundary of the back gardens of 2–14 St Margaret's Drive and the cul-de-sac Kenton Mews. The ashlar capstones on top of the wall were made from waste products of the gas and coke works in Bristol. Spent coke was smelted and poured into rounded moulds to make these distinctive and very hard wearing capstones. Ashton Park also has the capstones on much of its perimeter wall.

St Ursula's High School

During World War II much of the school was destroyed but it was rebuilt in 1948, mainly because of the determination of the Sisters. The uniform is navy and yellow. In September 1968 it was necessary to raise the School fees per term to £20 per term for Juniors and to £30 for Seniors. There were extensive additions and improvements to the building in 1972 and a sports hall was built in 1985.

In 1989 the Order of Mercy took the decision to withdraw from teaching to concentrate on social work. Once again parents stepped in and a new charitable Trust was formed in 1990 which purchased the school buildings, grounds and other assets from the Congregation of the Sisters of Mercy. The new board of Governors is responsible for the administrative and executive functions of the school. It was their intention to operate the School as an Independent Catholic Day School on a similar basis as at present, which will therefore permit the continuing education of children from all religious persuasions, both girls and boys up to the age of 16.

Mrs M. A. MacNaughton took over as Headmistress in January 1991 from Sister Cecilia when she and Sister Sebastian retired in December 1990. The Sisters have been associated with the school through its many transitions to the happy and attractive place it is today.

Springfield Kindergarten

The Kindergarten, for four to seven-year-olds, operated from 23 Kellaway Avenue, on the junction with Springfield Grove, from the 1930s until July 1970.

Miss Kathleen Thorne, previously with the Collegiate, which was then located off the top of the Downs, bought the house from a doctor. She became the principal, and with her Montessori training and helpful staff quickly filled a need in the area. Miss Thorne was known for her ability to play any piece of music by ear on the piano. The light, airy school went from strength to strength with many of the boys and girls passing entrance examinations for Clifton College, Clifton High School, Bristol Grammar or Colston's Boys' School.

Miss Thorne initially employed several part-time staff including Mrs Nancy Wollaston, from Liverpool, with a Froebel certificate qualification, who prepared the seven-year-olds for entrance examinations. Miss Rita Bishop specialised in singing, music and movement, Mrs Lawrence taught the four-year-olds and Miss Pagan the six-year-olds. Upstairs was extended to allow for extra children. There were four classrooms. The curriculum included reading, writing, numbers, singing, music and movement and handiwork.

A bottle of milk, containing approximately one third of a pint, was given to each child daily. The teachers took it in turn to stop the traffic in busy Kellaway Avenue – no zebra crossing then.

After Miss Thorne died suddenly in the Christmas holidays in 1945, Mrs Nancy Wollaston bought the school and became headmistress. The family moved there in 1947 having previously lived in Park Grove from 1939. Mrs Wollaston also became a Sunday school Superintendent at St Peter's in the time of Rev Langley Webb. When Mrs Wollaston retired in 1970 they were unable to find a purchaser for the school so the property reverted to a private house. Mr and Mrs Wollaston then moved to Winford, but later they returned, with failing health, to live in sheltered accommodation at the Good Shepherd Close, Bishopston. Mr Wollaston died there about a year later. Mrs Wollaston moved to a nursing home in Weston-super-Mare where she died aged 92.

PART 5
INNS AND FARMS

Inns

Cock o' the North

This purpose-built circular public house, located in Northumbria Drive opposite Waitrose, was opened in 1967 by Piper Milne of the Gordon Highlanders. The original inn sign depicting a piper of the Gordon Highlanders was unveiled at the time of opening by Mrs E. Boucher, wife of the Chairman of Courage (Western). At that time there were two bars named the Highland and the Lowland.

The name Cock o' the North comes from the Courage trademark of a cockerel and the location of Henleaze in the northern part of the city of Bristol. The Gordon Highlanders were also known as Cock o' the North so perhaps this was the reason for inviting Piper Milne to officiate at the opening?

The pub was renamed the Kebab and Calculator for an episode of the Young Ones, a cult classic comedy television programme of the 1980s.

Eastfield Inn

The inn, located in Henleaze Road, used to be a private gentlemen's club dating back to the early 1800s. It was then a much smaller building set nearer the road with a lean-to grocer's shop at the side. Close to the inn was a pump and letterbox. At this point the road became a lane with a stream running down one side.

From the 1870s to the 1880s the inn and the shop were kept by the Misses Harriet and Elizabeth Williams and their brother, Fred. Harriet was also a schoolteacher and Fred worked as an undertaker in Waters Lane, Westbury-on-Trym.

There was a bell over the shop door that tinkled when the door was opened, and on the shop counter was a large jar of black treacle. This treacle was dispensed by an ingenious system of weights, and one day when some children were playing with the weights, the treacle plopped out all over the counter! Many locals used to shop late on Saturdays and it was considered quite normal then to obtain the groceries at 8pm.

Eastfield Inn, *c*1932
This original inn and adjoining shop were demolished and replaced by the current
Eastfield Inn during the 1930s. (*Ray Pepworth collection*)

The inn was completely rebuilt in 1935. In the 1940s the ARP (Air Raid Precaution) had their headquarters in the skittle alley of the new Eastfield Inn.

Publicans included:

1871–85	Elizabeth Williams
1909–25	Frederick Williams
1928–37	Frederick Verge
1938	Lionel Verge
1944–53	Frederick Waymouth

Farms

The Briars (Henleaze Farm)

This attractive property, in Kenton Mews (off Henleaze Park), is shown as Henleaze Farm on the first Ordnance survey map of the area dated 1881. In 1904 Colebrook & Maddocks farmed here and in 1913 the occupier was shown as Sir J. Weston-Stevens. The Bennetts, a well-known local family, moved in here soon after and Mr Bennett used to drive daily, by pony and trap, past the Lodge House (now 12 The Drive) en route to his paper and stationery business in the city. In those days the road leading to the farm was a country lane and a stone horse mounting block is still outside the gates, having been incorporated into the existing pavement. The architecture of the Briars, now also known as 7 Kenton Mews, is very similar to Claremont House.

Green's Farm/Roper's Dairy/Clifford's/Express Dairy/ United Dairies

This farm was on the corner of the present Rockside Drive and Henleaze Road. Over the years most of the adjoining land was sold off and used for building houses and flats. Around 1920 Mr Roper liked the local children to visit one of his fields called the Meads at Wellington Hill West to play in the hay and toss it around to help the drying process. In those days the hay was left lying in the fields for some time before being stowed away or made into hayricks. In the 1930s Roper's cows roamed happily in the surrounding fields. The dairy had its own air raid shelter in World War II

Roper's Dairy, *c*1920
At the junction of Henleaze Road and Rockside Drive. The farmhouse has now been replaced with sheltered accommodation but the line of trees in the centre of the photos was cut down when Henleaze Lane was widened and the stream culverted to make the modern dual carriageway. Timbo, the dog, belonged to Mrs Simmons' family and lived in the cottage on the left. (*M J Tozer collection*)

that was also used by some of the locals. The dairy was known as Clifford's in the 1970s.

Following the closure of the dairy in 2001 an application made to build 21 flats and convert 244a Henleaze Road. The accommodation, with a day manager, is known as Ferndown Grange.

Henleaze Park Dairy

The farm that stood on the site of the present Esso Garage and Tesco Express was originally known as Henleaze Park Dairy. It was rented by the George Brothers from the early 1900s until 1921 from the Henleaze Park estate. Both Edwin, born in the late 1870s, and Henry had previously worked on the Henleaze Park estate when owned by the Derhams until most of the estate land was sold. They both lived in Henleaze Park lodges – 166 Henleaze Road (the thatched cottage) and 12 The Drive (opposite St Peter's Church).

Each June, in the early 1900s, the young George children were confined to the Park and the Paddock (then located opposite 12 The Drive) so as not to trample down the mowing grass in the other fields, where clover and moon daisies, scented grasses and their favourite 'shivery shakes' (quaking grass) grew undisturbed. Then about the middle of June came the great day when haymaking started – all by manpower and horses. In the evening, especially if rain threatened, neighbours came to help, including Frank Saunders and his brother Bert. The latter is shown in a photograph of 89 Henleaze Road. Most of the local men could wield a pitchfork and as soon as the rumour went around 'they're haymaking at George's', children came along as well. The game was to climb on to an empty wagon in the farmyard for the very bumpy ride to whichever field was being cut, clamber out and race back to the yard where the second wagon was being emptied. Tears and anguish followed at bedtime when Mrs George combed the tangles and hayseeds out of her children's hair. The George brothers were experts at shaping hayricks with one of them on top to scatter the hay as it was thrown up by pitchfork.

PART 6
ROAD MEMORIES

Audrey Walk

The *Bristol Evening Post* celebrated its sixtieth anniversary on 18 April 1992. It reproduced a copy of the 1932 edition, in which a 'well-built house with 2 receptions, 3 bedrooms, bathroom, white tiled kitchen and garage way' could be bought for £58 down and 17s 9d (88p) per week.

Brecon Road

Four new houses were built in Brecon Road, in the grounds of St Ursula's High School, in the 1990s.

Broadleys Avenue

The 1841 Tithe Map showed a field called Broad Leys in this locality.

Brookland Road

It was not possible to drive out on to Kellaway Avenue from this road until the 1960s although it was possible to walk through over the grassy mound. A resident still residing in another part of Henleaze recalls buying the one detached property in this road for £2,850 in 1950. At that time the road was not made up and there were only four houses there – one detached, two semis and a bungalow. Crest Homes added the houses on the former Bristol Cathedral School playing field on the other side of Brookland Road in the 1990s.

Cardigan Road

Grace's Stables, (Powles' Garage), (Henleaze Motor Care Company)
Alexander Grace had these premises built c1910 in Cardigan Road as private stables for his horses and carriages. Mr Grace was a well-known Bristol Quaker and owner of Grace's Flour Mills in Welsh Back.

Henry Powles, who came from Lincolnshire, managed the stables, transport and staff. When Mr Grace died in the 1920s, the executors offered the property to Mr Powles who had rented the premises from Mr Grace during the final years of his life for £2 per week. Henry Powles then became the owner of the property. He developed a private car hire business, operating seven-seater chauffeur-driven hackney vehicles, usually having six at a time. In the early 1930s the cars were mainly Austins, Austro-Daimlers and Buicks. In the late 1930s more modern Humbers, Hillmans etc. were introduced. Repairs had previously been carried out but this side was expanded when Robert Powles joined his father after serving his apprentice-ship at Bristol Motor Co. Ltd. During World War II some of the buildings were taken over by American Army personnel based in Henleaze, but the taxi service continued on a reduced scale, due in part to petrol rationing.

After serving in the Army for nearly seven years, Robert Powles developed the repairs side of the business further, including all body repairs. When Henleaze Park Garage (now the site of the Esso Garage on Henleaze Road) was demolished, the tyre business was re-established at Cardigan Road and the name Powles' Garages was used from the early 1950s.

Further expansion took place when Henleaze Motor Works (agents for Morris) closed and the partners recommended Powles' to their customers. (The site of Henleaze Motor Works on the junction of Cardigan Road and Henleaze Road was taken over by Gateway Supermarket in the 1960s.) Petrol tanks and pumps were added and a full forecourt service provided in the late 1960s.

Robert Powles traded until 1973 and then leased the property, goodwill and equipment to a tenant, B. J. Kington, who subsequently bought the premises in 1988. The Henleaze Motor Care Company was officially opened by Bristol's first black Lord Mayor, Councillor J. A. Williams J. P., on Wednesday, 27 March 1991.

Cavendish Road

In 1896 Henry St V Ames of Cote House sold the land that also included the roads now known as Henleaze Avenue and Henleaze Gardens to developers, and subsequently the plots were sold to individual purchasers. The houses in Cavendish Road were completed first. This road is included in the Henleaze Conservation area.

Claremont Court

Claremont's stables were situated at the top of Henleaze Park and were used as football changing quarters by the local schools before being renovated as housing and named Claremont Court.

Dorset Villas

These properties were built after Eastfield Terrace in the 1800s apparently to house artisans. Groomsmen used the stables at the rear for horses needed for the quarry work carried out on the Eastfield estate; there is still a mounting stone on the pavement.

Downs Park West

5 Downs Park West was advertised for auction in April 1949 by Lalonde Bros & Parham. There was a china pantry, a larder with glazed brick walls and marble shelves and a breakfast room which was also used as the maids' sitting room. Services included hot water circulation from a Beeston (AX) boiler in the kitchen with central heating radiators to the entrance hall and landing.

19 Downs Park West was advertised for auction in May 1921 by Chappell & Matthews. On the second floor one of the three bedrooms was fitted as a photographer's darkroom with a water supply. There was a carriage or motor entrance to the property and a separate entrance for tradesmen to servants' quarters. In the garden there was a full size tennis lawn.

27 Downs Park West was advertised for auction in May 1934 by John E. Pritchard & Co. The property, built around 1908, had four reception rooms, ten bedrooms, two bathrooms and offices in 1934. The detached double garage contained an inspection pit and there was a tennis lawn in the garden, a greenhouse and a summer house.

Eastfield

The first Eastfield properties were built in the early 1820s on land known as Eastfield Six Acres belonging to Sir Henry Protheroe of Cote House, Westbury-on-Trym. *Editor's note: just before publication I was able to view a considerable amount of historical paperwork relating to this area. Only an overview has been included because of time restraints. I do hope to elaborate further in the future.*

Eastfield Lodge

The Lodge was built around 1822 and the first owner, John White, moved in during January 1823. In 1843 it was owned and occupied by Joseph Davis, a barrister, who subsequently moved to Cotham and in 1863 it was the home of the White family. Mrs Marianne White was a widow by the late 1860s and lived there still in 1871 with three servants. The 1881 census shows the occupants as Henry Cooper, wine merchant, his wife, Edith and two young sons, Lyall and Philip. The 1891 census shows James Irvine, Captain with the Royal Engineers, his wife Nora and young son, John. In 1907 Sidney Humphries, a partner of Castle Flour Mills purchased the property. He was very prominent in Bristol public life in later years and was knighted in 1921. The Home Guard used the lodge as offices during World War II and kept ammunition (seven second bombs) in the cellars in case of invasion. Mr and Mrs Barrand, the owners from 1951 then sold the lodge to Mr and Mrs J. M. Ziman in 1964. Various members of the family have resided there from that time. Professor John Ziman F.R.S. (1925–2005) was an eminent theoretical physicist.

Arbutus Cottage

This property also known as 10 Eastfield was built around 1820 with additions made about 1870 of a kitchen, bedroom and bathroom. There is a strawberry tree (arbutus unedo) in the front garden. Since 1928 a walnut tree that fruits heavily every year has dominated the rear garden.

The Larches and Amelia Edwards

A stone plaque in the stone wall in Eastfield straight across from Grange Park commemorates Amelia Ann Edwards (1831–92) who enjoyed three separate careers: as a journalist, a novelist, and an Egyptologist. She lived in The Larches from 1864 to 1892. Amelia Edwards wrote a series of ghost stories for Charles Dickens, so perhaps he could have visited the area then?

The Egypt Exploration Society was founded in 1882 as the Egypt Exploration Fund by Amelia Edwards and Reginald Stuart Poole of the Department of Coins and Medals at the British Museum, in order to explore, survey, and excavate at ancient sites in Egypt and Sudan, and to publish the results of this work. Today it is one of the leading such archaeological organisations. For further information see http://www.ees.ac.uk/the-society/history.htm

Amelia's death in 1892 followed shortly after that of her long-time female companion with whom she had lived and travelled. Amelia's grave is in Henbury churchyard where it is marked by an Ankh and an obelisk. The Ankh was, for the ancient Egyptians, the symbol (the actual Hieroglyphic

Amelia Ann Edwards (1831-1892)
Amelia lived in the Larches in Eastfield from 1864 to 1892 (sadly bombed in 1941).
Amelia enjoyed three separate careers: as a journalist, a novelist, and an Egyptologist.
(*The Egypt Exploration Society*)

sign) of life but it is an enduring icon that remains with us even today as a Christian cross.

In 1892 the house was conveyed by Miss K. Bradbury to Mrs W. A. Greenslade and in 1927 by Mrs E. Greenslade to Henry Hosegood. The Larches was sadly bombed in 1941 and in the 1950s two new houses were built on the site.

Eastfield Road

An ice house was located at the end of this road – opposite Clark's Quarry – by the mini roundabout. The ice was brought up from Avonmouth by horse and cart.

The Polish Consulate moved to 132 Eastfield Road in 2005 from 132 Henleaze Road, formerly one of Henley Grove Lodges.

Eastfield Terrace

Limestone quarrying was the major activity in the area and these terraced houses were built around 1860 to accommodate the quarrymen on the Eastfield estate that included the adjacent quarry (now filled in and known as Old Quarry Park). Some of the houses have retained their original boot scraper built in by the front door. There are two stable buildings at the rear of nos. 11–15 that were approached through a double door entrance above no.15. In 1977 a hand pump was preserved in Eastfield Terrace.

In 1983 residents were concerned about the condition of the old civil defence building at the Eastfield Terrace end of Old Quarry Park. A block of flats, known as Pinefield, with a pedestrian entrance to Henleaze Road, was built in the 1980s.

East Medow Cottages

The rank of cottages located on Henleaze Road, opposite the Rockside Drive junction was built by the great grandfather of Mrs Crompton, the secretary at Henleaze Junior School in the 1960s. She also lived in one of the cottages. It appears that John Wilkins who married Alice Rose Ellis in

East Medow Cottages, 1964
Demolished in 1968. The plaque below the window shows their name and date of their build - 1834. (Meadow was formerly spelt Medow) (*Derek Klemperer collection*)

1900 stayed there during the first part of the century. The cottages had a plaque below the upstairs front window which read East Medow Cottages 1834. [Medow is now spelt Meadow.] The cottages were hit by an incendiary bomb in the 1940s. They were demolished in August 1968 and replaced by a small apartment block, Cranford Court.

Fallodon Way

The land on which 2 Fallodon Way was built in 1955 appears to have been part of the Northumberland House School orchard as well as a vacant plot from the 1930s housing development. A very old bramley apple tree in its back garden with a girth of 40 inches (1 metre) would have been in existence on the original estate here. The garden is separated from the Holmes Grove properties by an old grey stone wall which, according to old maps, would have been the boundary between the Northumberland House and Henley Grove Mansion estates.

The Furlong

These properties were built by Crest Homes in the mid-1990s together with nine houses fronting Brookland Road.

The cycle path that runs from The Furlong towards Sates Way was built in the 1990s when Tesco was built. However the 'white elephant cycle path to nowhere' still terminates at a gate and is only a few hundred metres long.

Golden Hill

Six terraced properties known as Golden Hill, off Kellaway Avenue, were built in the 1870s. Old deeds from 28 Golden Hill appear to show that swine must not be kept on the premises or tallow made there!

Grange Court

In the 1970s Durston Estate Agents marketed these 21 flats when they were new for £7,150 with the option of a garage for £250. Their brochure states that 'with electric central heating there are no fuel storage problems, no ash disposal worries, nothing to go wrong.' Owners of these two bedroom apartments were also given an electrical appliance of their choice up to the value of £150 from a list which included a split-level cooker, double-oven cooker, refrigerator, food mixer, freezer, washing machine, dishwasher and waste disposal unit.

Grange Court Road

Grange Garth, 19 Grange Court Road, the estate of John A. Bobbett deceased, was put on sale by public auction at the Commercial Rooms, Corn Street, Bristol by J. P. Sturge & Sons in June 1970. At that time there was a squash court in the double garage and an air raid shelter in the garden.

Harbury Road

Henleaze Business Centre moved into the former Co-op Supermarket in February 1990.

Henleaze Avenue

This was built on the plot shown as Twelve Acres on the 1841 Tithe Map and owned by George Ames who lived in Cote House on the Downs. When he died in July 1873 the land was passed on to Henry V St Ames who appears to have bought the land from his three brothers in November 1873 for the sum of £20,171-18s-0d (£20,171.90), plus a rent of one shilling (5p)

Henleaze Avenue, c1910
Only one lady pedestrian and no cars! (*M J Tozer collection*)

per annum. In 1896 the land was sold to J. Dole, gentleman, and H. J. Millard, contractor, for £16,500 and a rent of 6 guineas (£6.30) per annum.

Building then started in Henleaze Avenue and 4 (Ivydene) was soon ready and sold to Herbert Sidney Fielding and Alice Beatrice Mitchell for an undisclosed sum. Mrs Mitchell sold it to Genera Bridgeda Pitt in April 1936 for £700. Since then there have been various owners including Clee, McNab, and in 1991, Ryder. In 1991 local resident Derek Reynolds confirmed that his father came to live in Henleaze Avenue in 1898.

The ornate cast iron railings on the top of each stone wall were cut off and transported away by lorries to help the World War II effort. The stubs still remain on many of the walls. The corners of the pavement at the end of the road were broken by tanks en route to the tank park on the Downs where they waited to go to Avonmouth prior to the World War II invasion.

7 Henleaze Avenue

In May 1922 Chappell & Matthews were instructed by B. Allen Esquire to auction the contents (382 items). These included a hair mattress, Ewbank carpet sweeper, bundle of bean or pea sticks, a petrolite safety table lamp and a pair of oleographs.

Henleaze Gardens

In 1896 Henry St V Ames of Cote House sold the land in this area – which also included the roads now known as Cavendish Road and Henleaze Avenue – to developers. However Henleaze Gardens were not completed until 1901. Sheep were still grazing at this time on the Downs where houses were due to be built. This road has been designated part of Henleaze conservation area.

Henleaze Park Drive

Rosemary Shepherd (née Warne) grew up in Henleaze Park Drive in the 1930s and 1940s. Her father, Ronald Warne, was a well-known photographer in Bristol. He was too old for active service in World War II but, as a professional photographer, his photographs and films made an important impact in Bristol, particularly during the war years.

Her mother regularly attended Gill's, the hairdresser in Henleaze Road. When she had a perm her curlers had to be tied up with wires to the ceiling to obtain the right effect!

Rosemary attended St Margaret's School for two years, before going on to Clifton High School. After leaving school she completed a three-year Matron/Housekeeping course at Great George Street, Bristol. As part of the training she returned to Henleaze for eight weeks at Claremont School in the early 1950s. She subsequently worked at Cheltenham Ladies College for a year as a Matron, and then Badminton School, Westbury-on-Trym as a housekeeper.

Rosemary returned a few years ago to live in another house in Henleaze Park Drive near her former family home.

Henleaze Road

In 1921 the dual carriageway on Henleaze Road was constructed. In the 1950s traffic was a problem especially on August Bank Holidays. From about 6 or 7pm on Fridays and 4 to 5 pm on Saturday, it was nose to tail from Filton to Bristol Zoo on the Downs and often beyond until it dispersed for either Bridgwater or Weston at Ashton Gate. This was used as a bypass to Gloucester Road to avoid traffic going through the centre of Bristol.

Henleaze Lane
In the 1920s a small stream was culverted giving another road parallel to the trees resulting in a dual carriageway which is still used today. The Royal Blind School is on the right and Eastfield Quarry, (now Old Quarry Park) on the left. (*Simmons family collection*)

Henleaze Road, c1936
The shops have all put up their shades and there are far more cars in this view. The children from Henleaze Kindergarten can seen on the corner of Springfield Grove on the wide pavement outside their school. (*M J Tozer collection*)

39 and 67

The Sincock family moved from their shop at 67 to 39 Henleaze Road in 1916. The latter then looked out on to fields and the grounds of Springfield House. When it was Northumberland House School the daughters, who became Mrs Overton and Mrs Brooks, used to go to dancing classes there. They could remember the original shops which were knocked down to build a more modern rank from 73 (now Lloyds TSB) to 107 (the former Post Office, currently a St Peter's Hospice Charity shop).

177 – 205

This rank of houses was demolished in 1964 for the Jet petrol station. It was renamed on several occasions before planning permission was granted in 2005 for the demolition of the Total filling station and the construction of 22 sheltered apartments. The garage closed in April 2005.

249 (*Memories from resident, Mrs Simmons, 1990*)

I was born in my present house 249 Henleaze Road 83 years ago. My Mother lived in the area in Eastfield Road, near the Ice House and then in Eastfield Terrace before marrying my father.

Friday the Thirteenth (13 June 1952)
View from the Rockside Drive Junction of the 142 bus making its way to the Centre along Henleaze Road. Former quarrymen's cottages are behind the bus. The large pine tree was preserved when the block of apartments, Pinefield was built in the 1980s. (*K W Jenkins Collection*)

Mother's family used to take in laundry to earn a living. I was the only girl but had six brothers for company whom I loved dearly. I lived for some time with an Aunt in Westbury but I was not happy. Although I had everything I wanted I missed the company of my brothers and eventually ran away back to my mother – much to my Aunt's annoyance! I went to Westbury School – (now a community church) – and left at 14 which was the normal leaving age then. I can remember my father rushing out to pick up manure for his allotment at Canford after a horse had gone past. There was a huge beech tree which produced magnificent beechnuts at the beginning of the present dual carriageway but it was taken down to widen the road. Walnut trees lined the beginning of Lake Road and continued almost to the area now known as Glenwood Road. I've never tasted nicer ones from a shop!

Some of the old local houses have wells as there were a lot of springs in the area. In 1915 my brothers went to a horse fair, together with attendant steam roundabouts etc held on a field opposite Henleaze Avenue and behind Holmesgrove Road. (Now Holmes Grove)

I had many jobs, which included looking after children, being in service at the Blind School for seven years and also in private service in Redland. I got married in July 1940 at St Peter's a few months after my mother died. I then stayed on with my husband to look after my father, a veteran of the Boer War. My husband was in the Police War Reserve in World War II. We had sandbags in the passageway plus a stirrup pump and a bucket of water. He didn't like being in the house particularly when the bombs were dropping. We had several bombs nearby at Cheriton Place, Oakwood Road and East Medow Cottages.

Nos. 249–251 Henleaze Road, opposite Rockside Drive, built circa 1860 – before pavements – still survive. They have stones set into the walls to stop cart wheels causing damage.

Henley Grove

The father of Edyth Edbrooke (see also Downs Park School) bought 37 Henley Grove in 1927 and added the garage at the same time. Edyth lived there until 1971.

Kellaway Avenue

The Avenue was named after Mr F. C. Kellaway, who served as a Member of Parliament and Postmaster General. He was born nearby and took great pleasure in officially opening it in 1921.

In the 1950s the corner building at the top of Longmead Avenue, where Kellaway Building Supplies are now located, used to be the local Co-op store which also had a separate butchery department.

Kenton Mews

Planning permission was granted in September 1976 for six houses between the Briars and the last house in Henleaze Park and the widening of the access road to them.

Lakewood Road

Willowbank, sheltered accommodation overlooking Henleaze Lake with communal facilities, was built on the former tennis courts in 1979.

Lawrence Grove

In the 1920s Lawrence Grove became the access road to Henley Grove Mansion replacing the entrance adjacent to the former lodge, 84 Henleaze Road. The 1924 street plan of Lawrence Grove shows nine sites marked out on the north side of the road; none on the south side.

Lime Tree Road

In 1993 this new road leading to Tesco was named after the 40 semi-mature lime trees. In 1995 revised plans were submitted by Crest Homes for residential development of the Bristol Cathedral School playing field. Minor changes were proposed to the housing layout for 61 houses in The Furlong and nine houses fronting Brookland Road with landscaping and public open space.

Northumbria Drive

In 1991 Mr J. A. Tanner advised that no. 43, built in 1937 by C. R. McGill, had been a show house and the first property in Northumbria Drive.

McGill's also built the last houses – numbers 38, 40 and 42 – in 1966.

The library and Cock o' the North were developed soon after, closely followed by the demolition of the original Orpheus cinema. The latter was replaced by Waitrose with three studio cinemas above the store.

It appears that there was a pre-1940 agreement to have Northumbria Drive adopted by the City Council which included a stipulation that it should not become a bus route and prohibited access to the rear of the Downs Park East properties from the rear access lane. Both of these injunctions appear to have lapsed.

Orpheus Cinema

The original building was designed by architect Alec French and built by Stone & Co in 1937. It was a classic 1930s-style Art Deco building with an impressive façade, complete with a giant window at the front. Inside there was a marble foyer with stairs leading up to the balcony and the auditorium.

A local resident was taken as a child, by her parents, to the opening and to see the first film shown, *Lost Horizon*, starring Ronald Colman and directed by Frank Capra. As the audience entered the foyer they were all given a Milky Way or Mars Bar. There were 2,000 seats and tickets were 9 pence (3p) or 1 shilling (5p) for the stalls and up to 2 shillings (10p).

Early 1950s

The Saturday morning cinema shows for children in the early 1950s were well attended. One Henleaze resident recalls as a child having to pay 6d (2p) downstairs or 9d (3p) upstairs. The commissionaire was always very strict, but it didn't matter because there was always great cartoon and a western such as *Hopalong Cassidy*.

Late 1950s

Cinema audiences declined and the Orpheus, like many in the city, struggled to keep up-to-date with new technology. The cost of widescreen equipment was particularly expensive but proved to be a must as most people expected this new style of presentation.

1971

Audiences were at an all-time low and dozens of cinemas across the country were shutting their doors for good each month or converting into bingo halls. The Orpheus Cinema closed that year and the final film in this classic 1930s building was *Catch 22*, a fitting title for a cinema that had put up a brave fight.

1972

The cinema was sold off to the John Lewis Partnership and demolished. That could easily have been the end but local people campaigned for their cinema and won a partial reprieve. In the original supermarket plans the cinema would have disappeared, but due to public outcry Waitrose incorporated a new cinema in the building. It was too costly to convert the existing building for their needs so the supermarket consortium incorporated a three screen mini complex in the plans for the new building.

Late 1973

The Star Company opened it doors with a flurry of camera flashes and Miss Great Britain performing another opening ceremony on the Northumbria Drive site. One of the movies on show that week was the latest Bond film *Live and Let Die* – another apt title as by now the name Orpheus had temporarily disappeared. Audience numbers were still low, although the public of Henleaze and surrounding areas loved the cinema so much they kept it going with reasonable attendance.

1980s

The Cannon group took over and brought the cinema under the umbrella of a company that already ran the Whiteladies, the New Bristol Centre in Clifton and Bristol City Centre.

1994

It was reported that the Cannon Cinemas would close in November. A petition against its closure was started and was available for signature at the adjacent Dean News. The closure was subsequently avoided and the cinema remains open as the Orpheus, Bristol's only independent non-subsidised cinema with three screens.

Henleaze Library

Henleaze Library was officially opened at 11am on the 22 April 1970 and opened to the public at 3pm the same day. The library was an eagerly awaited new amenity to St Peter's Parish. It was designed by architects Miles & Wills and built by Henry Wilcock & Co. at a cost of some £30,000. The newly appointed Librarian was Miss Wendy Smart.

A total of 12 computers were installed for bookable free use by library members in 2002 and in 2006 disabled access and a meeting room at the front of the building was provided.

Oakwood Road Memories – Mrs I. M. Frost, 1985

I think I was the first resident of Oakwood Road, having arrived at number 32 in May 1932 with my husband and first child who was just twelve months old. Much building was in progress in those days, the 'straight' part of the Road was completed by the erection of eight houses nos. 30–37 by Allen Rayers.

I wonder how many people around can remember this, as numbers 30, 32, 34, and 36 were built in conjunction with the Bristol Electricity Board, as electrical show homes. Each house was fully furnished by one of four leading firms in the City, and throughout the four houses every type of electrical appliance which was then on the market was installed and on exhibition.

The houses were open to the public for one month. I should add that the exhibition was opened by the Lord Mayor, and a special newspaper supplement was printed. (These were the first show houses.)

Rockside Drive building was not quite complete at that date. Where the back gardens of Rockside Drive and Oakwood Avenue meet, there was a stream and footpath, which led down to the Henleaze Road, and I well remember the real 'country' type of one large stone slab stile still standing not far from where the bus stop now is.

There were several lovely elm trees, but they were lost to elm disease. The construction of other part of Oakwood Road (around the bend) was in progress, but there was no sign of houses in Hill View lower than Rockside Drive, or Hill Burn. This was all open ground where we wandered around and picked moon daisies.

Owen Grove

This was named after the Member of Parliament for Launceston, Thomas Owen, who lived briefly in Henley Grove Mansion in the 1890s.

A rare pillar box of the Edward VIII era stands at the junction of Owen Grove and Lawrence Grove.

Phoenix Grove

The name was said to refer to the emblem of Horfield Athletic Association.

Pyecroft

New roads built in the grounds of the former Blind School in the 1970s include Pyecroft, named after a field that bordered the present Hill View and Southmead Road. This field (reference 525) is clearly marked on the 1841 Tithe Map.

Remenham Drive

In 1997 a byelaw prohibiting skateboarding was passed and suitable notices were posted, where appropriate.

St Margaret's Drive

When St Margaret's School was demolished chalet bungalows were built here. In front of the wall now bordering Kenton Mews were the greenhouses run by Mr Hookings that were also demolished at this time. The houses from number 2 to 16 were continually finding broken pieces of glass in their back gardens for many years.

Daisy and Walter Nipper, the maid and gardener respectively of St Margaret's School, lived in a house known as The Cottage in the grounds. This was demolished in the 1990s and replaced by 18 and 18a St Margaret's Drive.

Southmead Road

In the 1920s there were just 112 houses in the whole of Southmead, mostly situated on the main road. However as most of these had front gardens Southmead Road was just a narrow lane then, just wide enough for two cars. The Post Office there doubled as a general store which always stocked chicken corn. In 1977 a new Police Station was built for the area at the end of Southmead Road, opposite the Fire Station.

Southmead Road *c*1930
Taken from the bottom of Hill View looking along Southmead Road. The Manor House is on the left, by the cars en route to Southmead. Waterdale House (demolished in the 1960s) is on the right. (*M J Tozer collection*)

Springfield Grove

In 1995 many local residents were concerned about traffic speeds and the increased traffic flow in 1995 (this is a road near the primary schools and used by many children) and as a result traffic calming measures were introduced.

Tennessee Grove

This road leads to the tennis courts to the east of Russell Grove. One reader suggests that the name is just a dreadful pun.

Walliscote Avenue

10 Walliscote Avenue, a semi-detached property, was completed in 1932 and bought by the Seal family for £750.

Wanscow Walk

The majority of the houses in this road leading from Park Grove to Henleaze Road were built in the mid-1920s. Until 1923 this area formed part of the Henleaze Park Estate. Wanscow Walk was named after Wansbrough's, the Solicitors, and Cowlins, the Builders. Walk appears to have been a shortened version of Horace Walker, the chocolate manufacturer, who was the third party responsible for the purchase of this land.

Waterdale Close

Number 7 was built on part of the orchard of Waterdale House. In the garden in recent years the remains of the ice house have been filled in and replaced with a raised flowerbed.

Waterford Road

Waterford Road originally finished at number 7 in the early 1910s. The area beyond which is now known as Grange Park and the roads leading off were all common wasteland with grass and bushes.

Wellington Hill West

This road was named after the Duke of Wellington who opened Horfield Barracks in 1837.

West Broadway

On the 1881 first ordnance survey map of the area Broadway Farm is shown in this locality.

Westbury Road

There is a preservation order on number 127 on the corner of Grange Court Road, formerly a Mercedes dealership. From 1908 until 1938 this property, although known as the tramways depot, was used only to house and maintain tramway taxis and stable overnight a bus that ran from Blackboy Hill via Henleaze to Filton. The local tram line operated on the border of Henleaze from 1908 across the Downs and along Westbury Road, but finished in Westbury village opposite the public toilets.

Wildcroft Road

In 1975 there was work on the small area of grass there to construct retirement flats (Wildcroft House) which included one one-bedroom flat, four one-bedroom flats for the handicapped elderly and a warden flat. On the plans there was also a laundry, common room, guestroom, spacious garage and seven parking spaces. This replaced part of the prefab site in the area.

PART 7

HENLEAZE ROAD BUSINESSES

Henleaze Road from 1905

(Courtesy of Kelly's Directories)
Researched by local resident – Heather Phillips, 1986
*Additional research showing the 2006 shops – Sylvia Kelly

In some locations the shop has not changed since the original research but others have located there during the two research dates. Finally any businesses only in operation between 1986 and 2005 have not been included.

In 1904 the Bristol city boundary extension took place. Before then Henleaze was listed under Westbury-on-Trym.

HISTORY OF HENLEAZE ROAD BUSINESSES

41.	1909	Britton's – butchers
	1962	Clarke's – butchers
		TV shop, Uplands Car Radios
	2006	***Whirlwind Videos**
43.	1915	Lenthall's Shoes
	1921	Collins – confectionery
	1924	Watson's – confectionery
		Nadim's – outfitters
	1966	Ford's – footwear
	1968	K G Stabb – shoes
	2006	***Bouckley's – hairdresser**
45.	1911	Bowkett's – ironmonger
	1921	Bowkett's – confectionery
	1924	Furber's – boot repairs
	1928	Watson's – confectionery
	1950	Hill's – confectionery
	1953	Adam's – confectionery
	1956	Need's – confectionery
	1966	Bartlett's – confectionery

		Alexander – confectionery
		Hyde Bain – optician
		Melsom Wingate – optician
	2006	***Newsom & Davies – optician**

47.	1909	Paxman's – dyers/cleaners
	1968	National Sunlight Laundry
	1973	Henleaze Jewellers
	1979	Hynam's – jewellers
	2006	***Hynam's – jewellers**

49.	1913	Newman's – greengrocer
	1956	Orchard – fruiterers
	1958	Jenkins' – fruiterers
	1966	John James – television
	1968	Turf Accountants
	1972	Mecca – betting shop
	2006	***William Hill – betting shop**

51.	1905	London, Glos. & North Hants Dairy Co.
	1921	Gilbert's Dairy
	1926	Hornby's Dairy
	1931	National Provincial Bank
	1972	National Westminster Bank
	2006	***NatWest – bank**

HENLEAZE ROAD BUSINESSES – CAVENDISH ROAD INTERSECTION

53.	1905	Shirley's – grocers
	1936	Civil & Military – stores
	1956	Bristol Co-op Society
	1960	Marjorie Weekes – dress shop
	1962	Quality Fare/My-store – supermarket
	1980	Boots – chemist
	2006	***Boots – chemist**

55.	1905	Charles Morrish – chemist/post office
	1911	Amy Morrish – drug store/post office
	1912	Blissett Howman – chemist
	1921	Mapson's – chemist
	1950	Boots – chemist
	2006	***Boots – chemist**

57.	1905	Lloyds – fishmonger
	2006	***Henleaze Florist**
59.	1906	Poultney's – butchers
	1960	Court's – butchers
		Ronto's – dress shop
	2006	***Ronto's – dress shop**
61.	1916	Thomas Bros. – electrician
	1921	Morgan's – ironmongers
	1964	Allen's – ironmongers
	1972	Stanton's – ironmongers
		Second to None – clothes
	2006	***Empty (late 2005 – Marks)**
63.	1905	Henry's – bakers
	1921	George Davey–confectionery
	1944	Cadena – cake shop
	1968	Caroline's – cake shop
		Mountstevens – confectionery
	2006	***Barnardo's – charity**
65.	1905	Eliza Collins – wine shop
	1916	Purchase & Co – wine shop
	1973	Roberts Wine
	2006	***Thresher – wine shop**
67.	1906	Sincock's – newsagents
	1919	also a post office
	1944	and library
	1956	Whittaker's – newsagents
	1960	Plowman's – newsagents
	1962	Beckett's – newsagents
	1964	Sully's – newsagents/china
		N S S – newsagents
	2006	***Forbuoys – newsagents**
69.	1905	Mrs Watkins – drapers
	1934	Lovell's – drapers
	1953	Baldwin's – coal merchants
		Swift's – cleaners

	1956	Lucille's – boutique
		Gateway Supermarket
	2006	**★Somerfield – supermarket**

71.	1914	Galpin's – motor cab proprietors
	1921	Slocombe & Hawker – motor company
	1924	Hawker Bros.
		Henleaze Motor Works
	1966	Gateway Supermarket
	2006	**★Somerfield – supermarket**

HENLEAZE ROAD BUSINESSES – CARDIGAN ROAD
INTERSECTION

| **73.** | 1931 | Lloyds Bank |
| | 2006 | **★Lloyds TSB – bank** |

| **75.** | 1925 | Thomas Cole/Bank Stores – grocers |

| **75. & 77.** | | Bristol & West Building Society |
| | **2006** | **★ Britannia Building Society** |

77.	1924	Lloyds Bank – moved to no.73 in 1931
	1931	Thomas Cole – china & glass
	1950	Mason's – grocers
	1958	Cole & Pottow – gents' outfitters
		Pople/Hodges
	2006	**★Pack of Cards – cards and stationers**

79. & 81.	1928	Leaches – fruiterers
	1944	Charlton's – greengrocers
	1962	Rileys
	1966	Jenkins' – greengrocers
	2006	**★Lloyds – greengrocers**

83.	1928	Parker's Bakeries
	1950	Witt's Bakeries
		Lucy's Larder
		Jaydene Fashion
	2006	**★ Jaydene Fashion**

| **85.** | 1930 | Hodders – chemists |
| | 1930 | Moss – chemists |

	1972	Henleaze Hardware
	2006	***Warriors – nail care**
87.	1931	Evelyn – dressmaker
	1937	Manty's Gowns
	1947	Betty Webb's – gowns
	1950	Young's – gowns
	1953	Elsa Mettem
		Snowden Travel
	2006	***First Choice – travel shop**
89.	1928	Albert Saunders – decorators
	1931	Midland Bank
	2006	***Betfred – betting shop**
91.	1930	Hornby's Dairies
	1962	Bristol Dairies
	1970	Henleaze Pet Shop
	2006	***Granite Transformations – kitchen worktops**
93.	1930	Tebbet's – music dealers
	1931	Marjorie – drapers
	1933	Williams Cooked Meats
	1935	A Johns – antique dealers
	1937	Bollom's – dry cleaners
	2006	***Johnsons – dry cleaners**
95.	1936	Ye Children's Shoppe
	1937	Mrs Murray Art Needlework
	1962	Mrs Foster's – wool shop
	1984	Henleaze Wool Shop
	2006	***Parsons Bakery**
97.	1936	Chain Library Ltd
	1960	Hales – hairdressers
		Paul's – hairdressers
	2006	***Chandos Deli**
99.	1936	Harvey's Cooked Meat Shop
	1939	Miss Stacey's – cooked meat
	1944	Webb's – cooked meat

	1960	Price's – grocers
	1968	F & A – furniture suppliers
	1970	Henton's Furnishings
	1973	Artefacts – linen shop
		Carpet shop;
		Cake shop;
		Patisserie
	2006	***Beauty Care**

101.	1936	Rowe's – shoe shop
	1958	Hembury – gowns
	1962	Harding – butcher
	1966	Young's – butcher
		Sweet's – butcher
		Callen's – butcher
	2006	***Henleaze Quality Butchers**

103.	1936	Voke's – builders
	1953	Dunstan Parsons – watches/clocks
	1956	Always – jewellers
	1973	Artefacts
	2006	***Treasures – gift shop**

105.	1938	Niven's – confectionery
	1944	Voke Junior – confectionery
	1950	Mrs Beyman – confectionery and post office
	1960	Golden Grill Restaurant
	1966	Silver Star Restaurant
		Toy Shop – Colston's
		Beauty Care
	2006	***Café Breeze**

107.	1936	King & Voke – automobile engineers
	1938	Passey's – motor car agents
		Malone's – confectionery
	1960	Fry's
	1962	Young's – stationery
	1968	Maby's post office
	1976	Colston's
	2006	***St Peter's Hospice – charity shop**

HENLEAZE ROAD BUSINESSES
– OPPOSITE CAVENDISH ROAD INTERSECTION

94. – 96. 2006   ***Avenue Cafe**

98.   **2006**   ***Gary Henri – hairdresser**

100.   **2006**   ***Your Move – estate agents**

100.   1934   Horace Davies – gents' outfitters
    1938   W H Davies – gents' outfitters
    1947   Cole & Pottow – gents' outfitters
    1958   Elliott's – solicitors
    2006   ***AMD Solicitors**

102.   1934   Caroline's – cake shop
    1966   Brookes – dry cleaners
        Julian Flook – wine shop
    2006   ***Boulevard Kitchens**

104.   1935   Mrs Peterson – confectioners
    1936   Miss Liddington – confectioners
    1964   Paskett Davis – confectioners
    1968   J D Cates – confectioners
        Eve's – gowns
    2006   ***Boulevard Kitchens**

106.   1935   Cavendish – hairdressing
    1960   Suzette's – hairdressing
        Bradford & Bingley Building Society
    2006   ***Parkhouse & Co – solicitors**

108.   1934   Verity's – costumier
    1947   Claud Pope – costumier
    1956   Elizabeth – ladies/children's clothes
        C J Hole – estate agents
    2006   ***C J Hole – estate agents**

110.   1934   Bristol Wireless
    1970   Bedec – wallpapers
    1972   Aspect – wallpapers
        Gateway Building Society

| | 2006 | *Tenovus – charity shop |

| **130.** | **2006** | ***Henleaze Dental Practice** |

HENLEAZE ROAD BUSINESSES
– DUBLIN CRESCENT & WATERFORD ROAD INTERSECTION

142.	1927	Henleaze Park Garage
	1968	Esso Garage
	2006	***Esso and Tesco Express**

| **144.** | | Auto Engineers |
| | **2006** | ***Esso and Tesco Express** |

146.	1928	Vowles – dairy
	1933	Broom's – dairy
	1947	Jago – café
	1950	Garden Shop
	2006	***Henleaze Garden Shop**

148.	1928	Miss Shapland – confectionery
	1930	Mrs Rogers – confectionery
	1953	Cowell's – confectionery
	1958	Cowell's Candy Stores
	1962	Lanes – confectionery
	1966	Candy Stores: Garden Shop
	2006	***Henleaze Garden Shop**

150.	1928	Mrs Millar/Millar's Ltd – draper
	1972	Henleaze Fish Bar
	2006	*** Henleaze Fish Bar**

152.	1927	Barclays Bank (moved to 158 in 1939)
	1939	Ball's – decorators
	1953	Neate's – ironmongers
	1956	Neate's – launderette
		Henleaze Sports Shop
	2006	***Henleaze Road Post Office**

154.	1928	Edyth – boot & shoemaker
	1955	Francis – boots & shoes
	1956	Trymvision – radios

	1962	Home Décor
	2006	***Distinctive Kitchens**
156.	1927	Gill's – hairdressers
	1962	Aimee – hairdressers
	2006	***La Boutique – beauty salon**
158.	1927	Hughes – builders
	1927	Ball's – decorators
	1939	Barclays Bank
	2006	***City Glass**
168.	1927	Barlett's – greengrocers
	1933	Miss Hort – wine & spirits
		Brooks Dye Works
	1937	Macdonalds – wine & spirits
	1939	Batchelors – wine & spirits
	1953	Collins
	1962	Coopers: Patco – wine shop
	2006	***Costcutter – convenience store**
170.	1927	Jefferies – newsagents
	1938	Gwilliams – newsagents
	1940	Nichols – newsagents
	1944	Organs – newsagents
	1970	Jones – newsagents
	1972	Mahon's – newsagents
		Hill's – newsagents
	2006	***Avonvale Electrics**
172.	1927	Western Boots & Shoes
	1950	Goodenough – shoes
	1972	Golden Gate – takeaway
	2006	***Golden Gate – takeaway**
174.	1927	A Jayne – provision dealers
	1931	Salter's – provision dealers
	1950	Bradley's – stores
	1960	Collinge Enterprises
	1966	Jury's – mini store
	1972	V G – stores

		Males Tools
	2006	**★Vivienne Taylor – beauty salon**
176.	1927	Godsell's – butchers
	1950	Harding's – butchers
	1964	Pruett's – butchers
	1968	Sellars – butchers
	1972	Sanders – butchers
		Bay Tree Wholefoods
	2006	**★ Bay Tree Wholefoods**
178.	1926	Brain's Grocers
	1938	Henleaze Cycle Exchange – Harvey's
	2006	**★Harvey's Cycle Exchange**
180.	1926	Miss Hunt's – drapers
	1960	Jeanette's Ladies Outfitter
	1968	Doris Cox – gown shop
	1985	Snippitz – hairdressers
	2006	**★ Snippitz – hairdressers**
182.	1927	Hough's – ironmongers
	1930	Willways Dye Works
	1950	McEwen – estate agents
	1953	Park Street Sweet Stores
	1958	Smith's – confectionery
	1962	Simmonds
	1984	Coronet Sweets
	2006	**★Maestri Jackson – hairdresser**
184.	1928	Reed's Watch & Clock Shop
		Waites Opticians
	1947	Hill Bros. – electrical
	2006	**★Huthwaite – building consultant**
186.	1928	City & District Fresh Fish Supply
	1962	Henleaze Fisheries
		North Western Estates
	2006	**★Clark & Co – estate agent**

188.	1928	Gazards – provision dealers
	1929	Higgs – confectioners
	1960	Roberts Bakers
	1968	Maxines Bakers
	2006	**★Hancock Masonry Ltd**
190.	1928	George Jones – greengrocer
	1935	Park Drive – fruit stores
	1972	Werretts – florists
		Smith & Webbs – greengrocer/florists
	2006	**★Ikon – school & sports**

LOCAL BUSINESS HISTORIES

Whirlwind Video – 41

This independent video store has served the local Henleaze community for the past 16 years. However, during recent years there have been dramatic changes in the film hire business; the trade has changed from 50% video and 50% DVD hire to mainly DVD hire and the independents now have to withstand competition from the big chains and internet so the emphasis is on understanding the needs of the customer. One of their windows acts as a community noticeboard for posters for local musical and theatrical events. Further information is available in the shop on their huge range of popular films – over 1,000 titles on DVD – and twice that number on video.

Newsom & Davies – 45

This independent optician practice was established in 1977. For many years it has supported unwanted spectacles for re-use in developing countries. For further information see http://www.newsom-davies.co.uk

Hynams, The Jewellers – 47

On 21 April, 2004 Richard and Vanessa Hynam celebrated the 25th anniversary of the opening of their shop. Richard was the last apprentice watch and clock repairer to be taken on in Bristol by the long-gone jewellers, Pleasance and Harper of Clare Street in the City Centre. After his training and several subsequent years working as a watch repairer, he

Henleaze Road Shops, *c*1920
Sincock's the Newsagents was also the Post Office with a post box outside. A wheeled cart containing a milk churn is parked in the road but it is safe enough for the little lad in his boater to tricycle along the gutter. The dairy in the far corner is now a branch of the NatWest Bank. (*M J Tozer collection*)

decided to become self-employed and started work on repairs for several Bristol jewellers. One of his customers was Henleaze Jewellers of this address. When the business came up for sale Richard, Vanessa his wife, with a baby and a three-year-old in tow decided to buy it. There is a box of toys in the shop to this day – for customers' children.

Henleaze Road Post Office – 55, 67, 107 and 152

The Post Office has moved four times in Henleaze Road.
1. Its first location was inside 55, the chemist shop, Charles Morrish.
2. Sincock's at 67 operated as a newsagent as well as a library but also took on post office responsibilities in 1919.
3. The move to Maby's at 107 was in 1968.
4. Colston's then took over responsibilities at 107 in 1976.
5. The Post Office then moved across the road to 152 after Mr Colston retired in 1998.

Lloyds (Greengrocer and Former Fishmonger) – 57 and 81

The first parade of shops in Henleaze Road (located between the existing NatWest Bank and Somerfield) was built in 1902. The first business to open was Lloyds, at number 57. The shop originally operated as a fishmonger and was run by Gabriel Lloyd who already had four other shops, two in Blackboy Hill and one each in Westbury-on-Trym and Cotham. The shop remained as a fishmonger until the 1970s, when David Lloyd, grandson of Gabriel, introduced some greengrocery. His son, Rob, became involved in the business which continued the movement towards fruit and vegetables and in 1984 the shop stopped selling fish. In 1988 the greengrocer at number 81 was taken over by Lloyds and, for a period, they operated from both sites. After a time number 57 became the Henleaze Florist and the greengrocery continued as Lloyds at number 81.

Poultneys the Butchers (Now Rontos) – 59

The building of the shop commenced around 1898. It was subsequently opened as a butcher's by Mr E. T. Poultney, Senior around 1905. In order to obtain some fresh stock for his shop Mr Poultney used to go to Claremont House to kill the calves with a pole-axe. The Bruce-Coles living at Claremont House owned a large yellow Buick driven by their chauffeur. On the rare occasions that Mrs Bruce-Cole went to the butcher's she did not have to leave her car; Mr Poultney would come out and receive her instructions standing on the pavement.

Les Meek started work as an apprentice butcher at Poultney's on 27 December 1929 at the age of 14, working for 12 shillings (60p) per week. As there was no public transport in Henleaze at this time (although trams were running to Westbury), he used to walk from his home in Southmead, over a stile by the Blind School (demolished in the 1970s and replaced by the Neo-Georgian development), passing Roper's Dairies (now replaced by the apartments known as Ferndown Grange at the junction of Rockside Drive and Henleaze Road).

Les Meek worked for three years before being entitled to a three-day holiday which had to be taken Monday to Wednesday. He worked a five-day week, but Monday and Wednesday were half days! After three years he received a rise of one shilling (5p).

It was normal in the 1930s for people to telephone their butcher just for one chop costing about 3d (1p) for same day delivery and Les used to deliver the meat to residents by bicycle. One day he took the corner at Henleaze Park and Hill View too quickly; his bike went in one direction, the meat in the other, while he somersaulted into a garden, but was fortunately unhurt.

Here are some 1931 prices:

2lb 11oz *(1,219g)* Beef 2s. 3d *(11p)*
1lb *(454g)* Beef sausage 9d *(3p)*
14oz *(397g)* Breast of Lamb 7·5d *(2p)*
1lb *(454g)* Cuttings (lean beef) 7d *(2p)*

Mr Poultney Senior retired in 1936 and lived until he was 96 years old. His son, Mr E. C. Poultney took over the business, retiring in 1957 when Mr Court bought the shop. In 1929 there were two other butchers in Henleaze, two in North View and several in Westbury.

Sincock's (now Forbouy's) – 67

Mr Sincock bought this property in 1904 and later ran it as a newsagent and fancy goods shop; he also ran two shops in Sneyd Park and Westbury-on-Trym. In the early 1900s the shop had a clear view across fields to Henley Grove Mansion. In 1919 the shop also became Henleaze Post Office. When the Sincock daughters left school they both went into the business. Mrs Brooks covered the accounting and Mrs Overton ran the library.

Hawker Bros (now Somerfield's) – 71

From 1924 Gordon Hawker and his brother were proprietors of the former garage on the corner of Cardigan Road. They were dealers for Morris Cars. Gordon died at the age of 99 in 1998.

The Bank Stores (next to Lloyds TSB) – 75 & 77

A local resident recalls visiting this shop, run by Mr and Mrs Cole, in the 1930s. There was always a gorgeous smell of cheese and bacon and the edges of the counters were always full of tins of biscuits. There would be a chair for customers to sit and place their order which was delivered later that day.

A.T. Elliott & Co (now AMD Solicitors) – 100

AMD Solicitors have practised continuously out of their Henleaze Road premises for over 50 years. There will be many residents who will recall

Powles' Garage, *c*1930
Located in Cardigan Road. Three limousines ready for a wedding with uniformed chauffeurs. (*Robert Powles collection*)

89 Henleaze Road, *c*1913
These cottages were demolished in the late 1920s. The Midland Bank occupied the new no.89 since it was built in the early 1930s until 2004. The school notice on the lamp standard refers to St Joseph's school run on the site of the present Leonard Hall until the early 1900s. The people are believed to be Mr and Mrs Bert Saunders and their daughter Molly. Frank Saunders, Bert's brother lived in the cottage on the right. Mrs Saunders was the local midwife and Bert was a builder and decorator. (*M J Tozer collection*)

the early days of A.T. Elliott & Co when the firm's founder, Tony Elliott, opened a small office opposite what was then Clark's butcher's shop in 1953 before moving to their present location at 100 Henleaze Road. Tony Elliott himself retired in 1986 but not before joining with Tony Moore (one of the present proprietors of the business) in Partnership. Tony continued to practice from 100 Henleaze Road ably assisted by his right hand man, David Jackson who is also a well known local jazz musician. In 1997 A.T. Elliott & Co joined forces with Arthur White Davies & Co of 43 North View Westbury Park and in 2001 the practice changed its name to AMD Solicitors, a clever use of the partners Anthony Moore and Marian Davies' initials.

Elizabeth's (now C J Hole) – 108

Mrs Alice Choules became the owner of Elizabeth's ladies and children's fashions in 1938 and was known to her clients as Elizabeth. The shop was taken over on her retirement by Mr Thorpe of C J Hole, estate agents. Charles Joseph Hole established C J Hole in Bristol in 1867 on College Green to collect rents on behalf of Bristol City Council. The company

108 Henleaze Road, 1970s
Elizabeth, ladies and childrens' clothes shop closed down. The notice in the right hand window shows that C J Hole, the estate agents will be opening there shortly. (*Anne Choules collection*)

grew extensively and has been passed on through the generations with the Henleaze office opening circa 1979. C J Hole offers a full range of estate agency services which still include rent collection, but now for private landlords, as well as auction and mortgage services.

Henleaze Garden Shop – 146/148

After John Stenner was demobbed in 1947 he decided to open a garden shop and rented 146 Henleaze Road. Before joining the army he had worked for a seed merchant. A coal-fired greenhouse was built on the garage side in order to grow plants to sell in the shop; the base of this can still be seen where the perennials are laid out at the rear of the shop. Cacti were very popular from the 1950s and soon the shop doubled in size when they decided to take on number 148 next door in the 1960s. Further greenhouses were also erected at the rear and used for producing cut flowers.

In 1950 John married Vera and she has been involved in the business ever since. Both their children, Jane and Robert, joined the business over 20 years ago. Mike Baker, who has assisted many Henleaze residents with their gardening problems, has worked in the shop for more than 40 years.

Harvey's Cycle Exchange – 178

The grandparents of the present owner came to 178 Henleaze Road in 1938. This family business had been established since 1919 for motorbikes as well as pedal cycles but after the First World War concentrated on pedal cycles.

Pre-war most of the employees at the Bristol Aeroplane Company cycled to work. A man could buy a three speed upright Hercules for £3-19s-6d (£3.98) which was the equivalent of two week's wages and many paid for this at the rate of 1 shilling (5p) per week. The Raleigh, a rather grander model, cost £4-19s-6d (£4.98).

To meet today's needs, the shop has a great range of bikes including elegant lightweights, mountain bikes, shoppers, as well as the latest for the kids and numerous accessories. The repair and servicing workshop on the premises is backed by personal expert advice.

Miss Hunt's (now Snippitz) – 180

One former Henleaze resident recalls four or five Hunt sisters who were very charming and small in stature. The family ran a drapery business here from 1926. The sisters went to church in a crocodile formation wearing panama hats. Many of the items in their shop included a farthing or three farthings in the price so the sisters often needed more farthings from customers and friends to ensure that the correct change was available.

Shop Memories

Janet Attewell-Smith, 2006
In the 1970s, newly married, I recall so many of the shops on Henleaze Road. Lloyd's the fishmongers was an open air shop with a slab of marble containing the daily catch. Woodcock were hanging at the side of the shop waited to be plucked. Clark's butcher's shop, tucked away at the top displayed home made faggots and the sweetest lamb chop.

Elizabeth's had knickers in brown boxes, vests for old ladies, socks packed in military precision and dresses that filled a rail in the back room. When I was strolling, proud with my pram I would sneak into Elsa Mettem's dress shop. The bell would tinkle but there was always a quiet coolness inside where the dresses hung behind voile to minimize disruption and dust. The green dress with lace was simply a must!

The aroma and the animals from the Pet Shop beckoned. There were bird bells and millet, straw on the floor, and various cages stuck by the door. I remember goldfish in bowls, gerbils, rabbits and sometimes baby guinea pigs.

We continued on to the Post Office which was also filled with toys. Andrew was there with meccano, sweets and lego for my boys. Finally we would go to Maxine's for meringues, coconut macaroons, battenberg slabs, or vanilla slices. No talk of five fruits a day! We were happy with pastry made the old fashioned way.

The shops in Henleaze Road were used by my great grandmother in the early 1900s.

A. G. Hookings, Henleaze Park Gardens, Westbury-on-Trym
Portion of Plant Houses.

Market Gardening, *c*1930

Mr Hookings rented part of the Henleaze Park Estate. The rear wall behind the greenhouses still remains and the large house behind it is Claremont. The front wall with the espalier fruit trees was demolished to make way for a wider road and the front gardens of the chalet bungalows in Henleaze Park. A continuation of the front wall remains and is the boundary between Kenton Mews and St Margarets Drive. The rear centre is now the location of Henleaze Infant School. *(M J Tozer collection)*

PART 8
CHURCHES

Henleaze & Westbury-on-Trym Community Church
History of the Building

One of the Westbury-on-Trym Parish Council Minutes for 1790 records the wish to build a school but also the lack of a suitable site. Two rooms in the Poor House were therefore used for the purpose.

In 1837 (the year Victoria became Queen) the decision was taken to build a Boys School, later known as Edmonds School. This building is now an office, situated round the corner in Eastfield Road. This area was known as The Butts, presumably because of its use for a firing range, or even archery practice.

On 4 May 1838 the Parish Council agreed to sell 'not more than a quarter of an acre of the Poor House garden for the purpose of erecting a school for girls.' The land was sold to the Feoffees of Edmonds Charity, which had been founded in the seventeenth century by Anthony Edmonds. The price of the land was fixed at £50.

The school appears to have been opened in 1840 (the year of the introduction of the 'Penny Post'). The building consisted only of the central portion of the present structure, with decorative carved stone windows.

The Girls' School had 45 pupils and the Mistress was rewarded with the princely sum of £31 p.a. However she did appear to enjoy the help of five paid female 'monitors' (believed to have been older pupils). The Infants' School Mistress was paid £32 p.a. to look after 83 young charges for six days a week, also with some assistants. These salaries included the 'children's pence' (fees paid before the Education Act brought in free schooling) which they apparently paid to attend school, and the teacher also had to provide coal for heating the building, presumably when he/she considered it necessary.

In 1846 the National Society made a comprehensive survey of all schools and these were included. The Edmonds Boys' School and the Girls' School were both used on Sundays as well as weekdays. The 52 boys in Edmonds Boys' were taught by one master who was paid £55 per annum.

The building was sold on 14 July 1855 (during the Crimean War) to the Parish Church of Westbury-on-Trym and was then called Westbury-on-

Trym Female School. The Boys' School was retained by the Anthony Edmonds Charity and was transferred on 12 December 1899 to the Official Trustee of Charity Lands which became the Official Custodian for Charities in 1960.

The Infant and Girls' schools appear to have been amalgamated at the end of the nineteenth century as the girls' building was enlarged twice and the extra rooms used for the infants. Note the 1901 inscription on the Eastfield Road elevation. The original building for the infants (still bearing the title, visible from Westbury Hill) was used in the 1920s by the pupils from Eastfield Road and Albert Place for woodwork and cookery.

The Boys' and the Girls' school buildings were exchanged with a property in Channell's Hill on 3 May 1967 and the schools were transferred there. The large cast brass War Memorial which had been installed in the Boys' School in the early 1920s was then transferred to the Girls' School building where it remains in the room used for church meetings in 2006.

The transfer was confirmed by an agreement dated 14 June 1972 when the property was conveyed to Bristol Corporation and valued at £7,625. The building was used as the Westbury Adult Education Centre until 1993 and then, after over a century and a half of use for the education of all ages from infants to adults, it was sold to Highgrove Church on 6 December for £60,000 and began a new and perhaps more exciting phase of its history as the Henleaze and Westbury-on-Trym Community Church.

The Church started here in 1993 with the aim of reaching out to and caring for the communities of Henleaze and Westbury. There are about 130 adults and 90 children who use the church which celebrated its tenth birthday in 2004. The Sunday morning services are at 10.30am to which all are welcome. For more details about the church visit their website: www.henleazechurch.co.uk

Sacred Heart Church

The Convent Chapel in Brecon Road was used by local Catholics until 1939. However, during the 1920s and 1930s there was a considerable amount of new housing in the immediate area and with an increasing Catholic population it was decided that a new church was needed and this was built by Stansell's from Taunton.

The Reverend Mother of the Sacred Heart Convent gave the Diocese a plot of land at the bottom of the orchard fronting on to Grange Court Road as a site for the proposed new church and presbytery. Included in the design of the new church was a concrete roof structure underneath the pitched tiles to withstand incendiary bombs and also seating for approximately 250 people. The foundation stone was laid on 18 March and the church was opened on 13 September 1939 by the Rt. Rev William Lee, Bishop of Clifton. The first Parish priest was the Rt. Rev Mgr. Cyril Hookway.

On 20 June 1950 there was a four-hour service for the consecration of the church. Three bishops and more than 50 clergy attended. The public were not admitted to the first part of the service because of the large number of participating clergy. They gathered in the grounds to watch Bishop Rudderham begin the consecration in the open air.

In the 1960s two occasions were televised in black and white from the church; in 1960 the baptism of Katherine Thomas and on Christmas Eve 1969, Midnight Mass.

Newman Hall

Stansell's started constructing the hall in June 1961 and it was completed a year later at a cost of £28,000. The new building was designed to seat 250 people in the main hall, with a fully equipped stage, dressing rooms, kitchen, lounge bar, library and first floor flat for the manager. It was officially opened on 22 June 1962.

A mural of characters from Gilbert and Sullivan operas was painted in the lounge bar by well-known local artist Frank Shipsides and unveiled by Donald Adams from the D'Oyly Carte Opera Company. This was particularly fitting as the hall became the home of Bristol Catholic Players for their annual Gilbert and Sullivan productions.

In 1983 Shears Construction carried out additional building work which included a new bar to serve into the main hall. The kitchen was enlarged and new toilets, including one for the disabled were provided as well as an internal access stairway to the Parish room on the first floor.

Newman Hall continues to be a popular venue for many varied and interesting local events.

St Peter's Church

Both the church and its semi-permanent building were designed by A. R. Gough FRIBA and built by Messrs William Cowlin & Sons and Messrs. Pratten of Midsomer Norton respectively. Services began in the latter building from 13 March 1926. The new parish church, St Peter's, in The Drive, was consecrated on Saturday, 29 October 1927.

The organ in St Peter's was built in 1869 by Henry Willis for Henry St Vincent Ames of Cote House, Westbury-upon-Trym. The organ was transferred from Westbury-on-Trym Village Hall to a gallery on the left side of the chancel in 1927 by Hele & Co. Ltd. of Plymouth after being purchased by the Trustees of the church.

Mrs R. K. Pagett, the widow of the first vicar, Rev R. K. Pagett, wrote the following in 1979:

> We moved into a flat in Henleaze (in Henleaze Gardens) in 1926 because the vicarage was not built. A hut that was used until the church was completed had a dual purpose. The sanctuary was screened during the week and the rest of the place was used for secular activities. St Peter's took 10 years to complete with three bays and a Lady Chapel added later. During World War II St Peter's Hall was used as a hospital.

The first few vicars were:
Rev R K Pagett (1926–36)
Rev J H Langley-Webb (1936–56)
Rev Edgar Wallace (1956–65)
Rev David M Sharp (1965–75)

St Peter's Church Hall

In 1940 the hall was used as a military convalescence hospital and wounded soldiers in their distinctive blue suits, white shirts and red ties were a familiar sight in Henleaze Road. The 227th Scouts (St Peter's Henleaze) regularly collected paper as part of the war effort but their paper store in the hall was officially commandeered as an air-raid shelter for the hospital.

Trinity-Henleaze United Reformed Church

The existence of the Church in Waterford Road is owed to the foresight of an Extensions Committee who established the church to serve the community gradually coming into being as houses were built in the new suburb of Henleaze. The Secretary of the Committee, Mr H. C. Wicks, cycling along Henleaze Lane – now Henleaze Road – one Saturday afternoon, saw a building and some land for sale. This was purchased, and Sunday evening services began in St Joseph's, a former Convent Day

Henleaze Congregational Church, 1906
(*Samuel Loxton collection*)

School. This building is now known as Church House. The church was designed by Frank Wills; it is spacious with aisles and an organ chamber. Today it is entered by a modern door in Waterford Road. The main church building was opened in 1907 as the Henleaze Congregational Church and the congregation then had a regular minister. In the 1920s the City Council decided to widen and improve Henleaze Road, and this necessitated cutting off a considerable portion of the school room.

One of the 1989 members living in Henleaze saw, as a little girl, the laying of the foundation stone. Two members who had a significant effect on the life of the church were Mr and Mrs Hampden Leonard who looked after the Sunday School – now Junior Church – for many years. Mr Leonard was also a generous Church Treasurer. The hall in Church House was named Leonard Hall in their memory.

An area between Antrim Road and Waterford Road was designated for a hall for the Church, but because of World War II in the 1940s the building was delayed until the 1960s. However the caretaker of the Church used it as a vegetable allotment for the war effort. There were many blackcurrant bushes as well and neighbours were invited in from time to time for a PYO (Pick Your Own) session.

In 1991 the Church arranged a recital to inaugurate their new Yamaha grand piano (a gift). This recital was given by Dr John Bishop, their then organist and a fine musician. Elizabeth Herring, one of The Henleaze Society committee members was present at the recital and was thrilled by the occasion. She conceived the idea of arranging a concert for The Henleaze Society in the church. The Church Elders had just completed a refurbishment of the building and a marvellous acoustic was discovered, which led them to put on, from time to time, concerts of varying styles, but often with a classical music programme.

The Henleaze Society hired the church for three concerts in 1992, 1994 and 1996. Each programme was built around musicians, young and old, who lived in Henleaze or were connected with the area. The Henleaze Concert Society was then formed by the Minister, Rev Bernard Chart and others around the Emerald Players, led by Roger Huckle.

In 2002, Henleaze United Reformed Church was approached by the members of Trinity United Reformed Church (Cranbrook Road, Redland), with a request that the two congregations join together to form one united church. Having considered the future, the position of the church in the local community, the on-going cost of maintaining a large building, and the fact that nearly half of the Trinity members lived closer to the Henleaze church than Cranbrook Road, they decided that a union would bring new life and opportunities.

Both the Trinity church and the Henleaze church were without a Minister at the time. The Elders elected a small committee to discuss the details of a union; the decision to unite was approved by both Church Meetings. The Bristol District Council of the United Reformed Church supported the proposal.

On the 13 October 2002 the united church, Trinity-Henleaze United Reformed Church, was formed and celebrated in worship. With a membership of near 200 people, and a junior church numbering 50 children, the new united church looked forward. A minister, the Reverend Tracey Lewis, was appointed a year later.

During 2005 the Trinity Church buildings in Redland were sold. Trinity-Henleaze United Reformed Church drew up plans to redevelop the church's community buildings. Rev Tracy Lewis invited The Henleaze Society, users of the buildings and people from the local community to contribute their ideas and to look at and discuss the new plans for the Trinity-Henleaze United Reformed Church which included:

- Replacing Waterford Hall.
- Linking the new building to the Church.
- Linking the Church and Church House.
- Improving the domestic facilities in all of the buildings.

106

PART 9
WORLD WAR II MEMORIES

Air Raid and Morrison Shelters

During World War II the Reed family who lived at 135 Henleaze Road slept in their air raid shelter in the garden whether there was an air raid or not as it was big and they had made it comfortable.

Morrison shelters were small bomb shelters designed to be used inside the house to protect families from enemy air raids. They were six feet six inches (two metres) long, four feet (nearly a metre and a quarter) wide and two feet six inches (three quarters of a metre) high. When not needed as a shelter they were often used as a table.

Mr Broome, the dairyman, lived at 146 Henleaze Road (now the Garden Shop), with his family consisting of his wife, their four teenage children, and his parents. They had a Morrison shelter in their living room. On 16 March 1941 there was a major air raid lasting most of the night. This raid, by 167 aircraft, hit parts of the centre which had previously escaped. The noise was unbelievable and in the middle of it all Mr Broome rushed across to the house opposite – 135 Henleaze Road – to ask if he and his family could share their purpose-built larger shelter.

'After the raid there was an eerie silence. The night sky was awesome, just one mass of red from the fires in the city.'

Rosemary Shepherd (née Warne) recalled air raid shelters in the area including 21 and 24 Henleaze Park Drive and could also remember that one of her neighbours had a Morrison shelter with wire netting on three sides which was used as a kitchen table when there were no raids.

There was a large public air raid shelter opposite the Henleaze Park Drive junction where Studland Court now stands.

The Americans

During World War II, around 1942, American soldiers were billeted in private homes in Shirehampton, Henleaze and Westbury-on-Trym. The Downs and parts of Ashton Court estate became parks for tanks, trucks and artillery. In Henleaze the Americans were billeted in many roads, including Lawrence Grove, Downs Park East and Cavendish Road as well as Badminton School.

At the time there was much criticism of the Americans taking over requisitioned properties in the area. There were hundreds of raw conscripts from the Deep South, many of whom had never worn boots before let alone lived in a large city. Some had never lived in stone houses with drains and did not know how to flush toilets. Many had spent two months at sea packed in ships, some were in transit to the Pacific and the Far East. On arrival here they received 90 days pay – a colossal amount of money. It was not unusual for a conductress on a bus to be given a pound note for a three pence (1p) fare and told to keep the change. Most of the shops were empty but Harvey's in Henleaze Road was a popular venue for the purchase of bikes. The Eastfield Inn was drunk dry and often had a closed notice on the door owing to the shortage of alcohol.

Their British comrades often resented them; in 1942 a British private soldier was paid around 14 shillings (70p) a week, whilst his American counterpart received three pounds, eight shillings and nine pence (£3.44.) Girls, many of whom travelled down from London, were strongly attracted to the American soldiers and British men often resented the way the glamorous Yanks impressed the womenfolk; one local nickname for girls who went out with Americans was 'spam-bashers'. Possibly some reference to the way having some nice young American lad might improve the family rations?

Elderly residents recall these wealthy, well-groomed glamorous GIs sweeping local women off their feet ('oversexed, overpaid and over here'). Many young women were thrilled at the presence of these tall, polite young men who spoke just like Hollywood stars and seemed to have endless supplies of chocolate, chewing gum and nylon stockings.

Every night the ladies of the United Reformed Church ran an evening canteen in the Leonard Hall for the servicemen. Tea and coffee was served and also some sandwiches, but most of their customers were the American servicemen who had nowhere else to go. These evenings often included singsongs.

The site of the present Esso Garage opposite was used as a maintenance depot for their vehicles. Most of the servicemen working there wore casual clothes and were known as GDs (General Duty) personnel.

ARP Rattles

These noisy wooden rattles were used when an air raid was imminent. Ray Pepworth is the proud owner of one.

Dad's Army
During World War II air raid wardens from K group in The Crescent were ready to deal with fires and incendiary bombs and to carry messages by bicycle. (*M J Tozer collection*)

Dad's Army

39 Henleaze Gardens was used as the headquarters of the 66th Searchlight Regiment (5th Gloucestershire Regiment) from 1939–41 under the command of Lt-Col. Mervyn Cook. Dad's Army had many night alerts, spies and mock attacks to contend with during this period. Later the headquarters were moved to Badminton School.

Daylight bombing raid in the 1940s

During a daylight bombing raid a bomb was dropped near Gill's, the hairdressers, at 156 Henleaze Road (now La Boutique). The blast blew out the plate glass window of the salon. Had the window blown inwards there would have been some nasty injuries to staff and clients who were there.

Empty Houses

Many old people were scared stiff by the air raids in World War II. Some moved to the country to stay with relatives. Houses were impossible to sell at this time and so many in Henleaze were left empty.

Homes Bombed

54 and 56 Cheriton Place suffered direct hits and were completely flattened by German bombers on 3 April 1941. No deaths or injuries were sustained in spite of all the devastation and the family was recovered from the Anderson shelter which was partially buried under all the debris. A Wolseley car was thrown across Eastfield Terrace by the blast from the direct hit to these houses. It landed on an empty bed of the front bedroom of the Saunders' family of what was then 3 Dorset Villas.

Cheriton Place
Clearly shows the devastation of the German bombing raid in April 1941. Numbers 50 and 52, in the centre of the picture, were built by local builder Len Watts in 1934. They suffered amazingly little damage considering they were right next door to the semis, 54 and 56 that received a direct hit - on right of the photo. (*Jim Facey collection*)

Local Police Constable Injured

William Fowler, a war reserve constable, was interviewed in 1991 for *The Henleaze Book*. He lived in Laurie Crescent in the 1940s. During World War II the constables were required to go into public houses, in pairs, to make sure there were no under-age drinkers. The constables also had to check lanes, military property and young woman out on their own. He recalled an incident at the rear of a house in Henleaze Gardens occupied by American soldiers in the 1940s. He had spotted a young girl in the garden, asked her to show him her ID and enquired what she was doing there.

Suddenly he felt a blow to the back of his head, possibly from a torch. He dropped everything and then felt a second blow from a metal instrument. He turned around to catch his assailant whom, he believed, was an American soldier. A struggle ensued and further blows to his head and shoulders prevented him from blowing his whistle for help. The soldier ran away and William, minus his spectacles and bleeding profusely, staggered down to Westbury Road where he was found by two special constables and taken to the warden post at the Orpheus for medical treatment by Dr Mabel Potter who happened to be on duty then.

He had to have six stitches in his head and was kept in the BRI (Bristol Royal Infirmary). Many of the staff there did a double take when they saw that the name of his consultant shown on a label above his bed was Dr Potter, a leading gynaecologist!

The Luftwaffe

On 25 and 27 September 1940 the Luftwaffe eluded British air defences and made two daring daytime attacks on the Bristol Aeroplane Company at Filton. The first attack was a great success: the second incurred heavy losses when caught by Spitfires and Hurricanes.

Recalling the former date in 1991 Philip Watts mentioned that a measure of prowess in his family was to ride a bicycle (no gears) from Henleaze Road, up Wanscow Walk and Park Grove to their home without dismounting. His mother, who was not athletic, had been shopping that morning. The siren had gone but they had not taken much notice, because it normally meant no more than a reconnaissance aircraft somewhere over the Bristol Channel. It was nearly midday and suddenly all hell was let loose. When Philip's mother looked around she saw 'all those planes with nasty black crosses on them' en route to Filton chasing her up Wanscow Walk which she took as a personal insult. The raid is one of those exhaustively described by Kenneth Wakefield in his book *Luftwaffe Encore*.

Pennies from Heaven?

Ray Pepworth recalled in 1944 accompanying his mother along Henleaze Road from the Downs with his baby brother who was in a huge pram. Some of the houses had been requisitioned for troops and as it was a sunny afternoon many of the Americans were sitting on the window sills and waving to passers-by. Suddenly they started throwing English coins into the large pram. Many of the coins missed and Ray rushed around gathering them up. His brother in the pram was unhurt by the shower of coins. Why were the Americans doing this? The next day they were going away and didn't need English money; they didn't know where at the time, but the date was June 1944. A few days later the D-Day landings in France began.

Pig Bin Collections

Part of the World War II effort included a deep large biscuit tin wired to every third tree in which residents placed old meat bones and skin that were subsequently used for glue. Households were issued with small galvanised bins with hinged lids for this food waste and a lorry came around twice a week to empty them. The smell was awful in the summer and the cats were always trying to eat the remains. Mrs Reed, a former Henleaze resident, kept her bin, marked B.C. (Bristol Corporation), on it in pristine condition during and for many years after the war. Gwenith Hewlett (née Reed) donated her mother's bin to the Imperial War Museum in 1992 to complete their pig bin collection.

Prefab Sites

Thousands of prefabs were built under the Temporary Housing Programme (1944–49) announced by Winston Churchill, particularly in the heavily bombed cities such as Bristol, as a short-term solution to a national housing crisis all over Great Britain once hostilities had ceased. The programme provided large numbers of houses quickly and economically to meet the needs of families whose homes had been destroyed by enemy bombing. It also provided houses for key workers who would be needed to help the country recover after the war as well as members of the armed forces returning home.

German prisoners of war laid the brickwork and foundations for many of the prefabs in Henleaze. Residents recall the prefabs being brought to their Henleaze locations in sections on large lorries.

These prefabricated buildings were well designed, with a hallway, a living room, two bedrooms, an inside fitted bathroom and heated towel rail, hot and cold running water, a fitted kitchen with a built in refrigerator and a gas or electric cooker. They were occupied mainly by young couples who kept their gardens beautifully. The prefabs were only meant to last for up to 10 years but they were very durable and proved ideal homes in many areas for more than half a century. Some people subsequently bought their prefabs and spent thousands of pounds renovating them.

In the 1970s the local council decided to remove the prefabs from Henleaze and replace them with permanent housing. However in 1976 it was reported that there was a delay in the development of the sites although empty houses were being rapidly removed. There were three prefab sites in Henleaze:

The Northumberland House site

In 1977 the planners advised that the site would be completed in three phases; approximately 133 dwellings to include some sheltered accommodation to be built in the early 1980s followed by a further 117 dwellings at a later date to be advised. The Henleaze Society pointed out that approximately 250 dwellings would be replacing 139 prefabs!

When the new properties were built Remenham Drive was divided into two with no-through vehicle access; the part to the east was named Remenham Park. Brean Down Avenue was altered so that there was no-through vehicle access from Fallodon Way to White Tree Road. Fallodon Court was created with sheltered accommodation and new dwellings were also built along part of Fallodon Way and Wildcroft Road. In White Tree Road an integrated development for disabled people with warden's accommodation and parking on behalf of the John Groom Housing Association replaced the prefabs in the late 1970s.

Henleaze Road site

The prefabs erected after the war (opposite Henleaze Park Drive) were replaced by sheltered accommodation, Studland Court, in the early 1980s.

Grange Park site

From the mid-1980s sheltered elderly persons' dwellings and 2/3 bed houses and bungalows replaced the prefabs in a new road, Grange Close North (leading off Grange Park).

Ration Books

These are quantities listed in a World War II ration book. Approximate gram and litre equivalents are inserted, where applicable.

Bacon and ham	4oz *(100 grams)*
Butter	4oz *(100 grams)*
Cheese	2–6ozs *(50–150 grams)*
Eggs	1 small every four weeks
Eggs (dried)	1 packet every four weeks
Margarine	2oz *(50 grams)*
Meat	1lb *(454 grams)*
Milk	2–3 pints *(1–1.5 litres)*
Sugar	12oz *(300 grams)*
Sweets	12oz *(300 grams)* every four weeks
Tea	2oz *(50 grams)*

Bread on ration, 1947
There was still rationing, including bread, as the centre stand in the former cake shop window at 63 Henleaze Road clearly shows (Barnardo's Store in 2006). Girls from St Ursula's: right to left, Stella Wilmott, Madeleine Greenaway and Sally Bower.
(*Greenaway collection*)

Unexploded Bombs

Unexploded bombs were recorded on 4 April 1941 at 31 and 37 Hill View and 53 Oakwood Road.

A bomb dropped on the tennis courts behind 28 and 30 Henleaze Park Drive. Fortunately it did not explode but it did leave a large hole adjacent to the tennis courts. Once the bomb was made safe a party of children and remaining men in the area brought along spades and had a fill-in party. Ronald Warne had bought one of these tennis courts and grew fruit and vegetables on it – they were not affected by the unexploded bomb.

Red Maids' School, 1940s
Miss Walpole, the Headmistress taking time out to relax with afternoon tea on the terrace. Note the sandbags by the window. (*Red Maids' School archives*)

PART 10
OPEN SPACES AND OUTDOOR SPORTS

David Thomas Tennis Club

The Club was located in Russell Grove. When the membership started to decline in the 1960s it was decided to sell off the land for the development of the housing which is located at the head of the cul-de-sac.

Golden Hill

The Romans left us one small memento. In the Bristol City Museum, there is a small bronze figurine of the god Mercury, only about two inches high (five centimetres) that dates from around 150AD. According to the records in the Museum he was found by chance in 1935 by H. G .Bryant whilst uprooting a tree in Kellaway Avenue. He is a sturdy little chap, full of detail from his helmet to his winged ankles. The Archaeology Department of the Museum state that there are no records of any Roman building or development on Golden Hill.

Tribute to Golden Hill – Sylvia Kelly (1987)

In the glorious year when Golden Hill was once again threatened by development it was so neglected by its current owners that the wildlife burgeoned. The fields are a short stay away along a lane full of 'weeds' and Speckled Wood butterflies that I went there every spare minute.

One day I met a small Skipper darting out from a leaf to defend his tiny bit of air space, looking sideways at me with enormous eyes. His wings were burnished orange, behind him the games pitches were full of shining buttercups, the haws had a blinding sheen, and there was every kind of ladybird making a living on the nettles. I tried photography but the film could not capture the great rich muddle of wildlife, so it was a challenge to try and find another way of representing something of its essence before it vanished.

It seemed appropriate to use bits of plants that could be found around the fields: that meant finding a small and distinct symbol for each tree and cutting grass stems to represent the surrounding buildings. It seemed right to use buttercup petals for Golden Hill and sprigs of herbs for the allotments. Before the map was finished, all my carpets had an underlay of drying herbage and I even had to iron extra petals!

Whenever I was working on the map, I could smell harvest in the fields and imagine the men who once farmed them. In that good summer, the incessant chirp of grasshoppers was evoked by the rustle of dried grass stalks. Plaiting red-brown bract together to make hedgerows was almost like laying the hawthorn itself!

Of course this flat effigy will always be a record of what was once present in Golden Hill, but I wonder whether we have the right to remove that Skipper's air space, to obliterate the communities that live in the nettles or to fell the trees. The living, moving things are what really matter, and they should not have to be condensed into a collage to make people appreciate their value. We should be using unremarkable urban habitats like this that are right on our doorstep, to open the door on a world of natural wildlife delights for many a modern child.

Aerial view of Golden Hill
Believed to have been taken in the 1930s. St Margaret's School is in the centre surrounded by trees. Claremont is to the top right. The triangle at the top of Hill View and Park Grove is clearly shown at the bottom centre. (*YMCA archive collection*)

1965

The first part of Ridgehill, situated at the top of Henleaze Park Drive, was built on the tennis courts and adjoining land formerly owned by the YMCA.

1973

In March 1973 the *Bristol Evening Post* stated that 'a £1 million plus land battle is looming over 22 precious acres (nine hectares) of Bristol's Golden Hill district. Residents have swung into action and hundreds of them have signed a petition to save the playing fields.' Henleaze Neighbourhood Society (now The Henleaze Society), has been actively involved in retaining this open space from the time it was created in 1973.

1974

On 18 March 1974 approximately 300 people attended a Henleaze Neighbourhood Society meeting in Henleaze Infant School about the future of Golden Hill playing fields. A report followed on 19 March in the *Bristol Evening Post* stating that the meeting was overwhelmingly in favour of Golden Hill being retained as an open space. Members were circulated with details of the CPO (compulsory purchase order) placed on part of the land by Bristol City Council. However Avon County Council opposed the development of the land. The Society understood that if this local government deadlock was not resolved the matter might go to the Secretary of State. Members were encouraged to write to the Minister before the 3 May expressing their opinion.

1975

Public enquiry (22–30 July) – Council House, Bristol. HNS prepared a statement for the Inspector, based on the results of their 1974 question-naire. The majority of HNS members were in favour of retaining these 29 acres (12 hectares) as open space, preferably a public park. At the end of the formal part of the enquiry the Inspector spent an afternoon touring the Golden Hill site and examining the lack of amenities in the district.

In October the Inspector's report included the following:

> I am of the opinion that Bristol Council's planning appeal should be dismissed and its compulsory purchase order not confirmed. This housing should not be permitted at the expense of maintaining an adequate level open space and recreational facilities. It is now a splendid ground with an exceptionally good pavilion and changing accommodation. Its size and visual attractiveness and the fine views

from it make it a valuable and obviously valued amenity in the area. Withholding permission does not of course ensure that this land will become available for public recreation and it does mean that such an outcome remains a possibility.

The Secretary of State agrees that the 3·4 acres (one and a quarter hectares) owned by the YMCA should be residentially developed but he considers that the proposed development does not fully utilise the potential of the site. It would help to meet the general need for smaller dwellings at lower cost if this could be achieved without detriment to the amenities of the area.

1977–78

The YMCA, after receiving planning permission for 46 houses in 1977, sold 3·25 acres (one and a quarter hectares) of its playing fields for development. 46 houses were built in 1978 in a development known as Golden Park that included Sates Way and the remainder of Ridgehill.

1986

Bristol Municipal Charities, which owned Bristol Grammar School playing fields, combined with Bristol Cathedral School in launching a scheme to develop the playing fields. It included housing on the whole of the Cathedral School's playing field – 6·28 acres (two and a half hectares) – a supermarket of 55,000 square feet, with car parking for 550 vehicles on part of the Grammar School's playing fields – 6·5 acres (two and a half hectares). The intention was that the Cathedral School should then take over the remainder of the land for use as its own playing fields. The proposal represented a loss of no less than 45% of the playing fields. The plan indicated the proposed supermarket immediately adjacent to Lansdown Terrace.

There was a tremendous amount of local opposition to these proposals on the grounds of the immense increase in traffic which would be generated, the resultant noise and air pollution problems, highway access and, above all, the serious permanent loss of the amenity. The area was zoned as private playing fields and, in the view of Henleaze Neighbourhood Society; it was felt that it should continue to remain so. The Golden Hill Residents' Association, with its membership of 450, held similar views.

1987

The Secretary of State decided to take the issue out of Bristol City Council's hands because of the nature of the proposed development of

Bristol Grammar School, Bristol Cathedral School and YMCA playing fields. However, Avon County Council had previously rejected the proposals to develop the grounds on the grounds that they would generate substantial traffic movements on and off Kellaway Avenue and in the residential roads in the area and that the proposals were contrary to the County Council's Structure Plan and would create unacceptable additional hazards to road users in the area. Avon County Council had also issued a directive to Bristol City Council requesting that permission to develop be refused. The proposed housing development Public Inquiry for the YMCA playing field due to take place in June was postponed at the YMCA's request

The Henleaze Neighbourhood Society distributed a questionnaire to residents living in the vicinity of the playing fields. The results were analysed and were presented on behalf of the Society at the Public Inquiry relating to the proposed supermarket complex on part of Bristol Grammar School playing fields and the proposed housing development on the whole of Bristol Cathedral School playing field which took place between 15 and

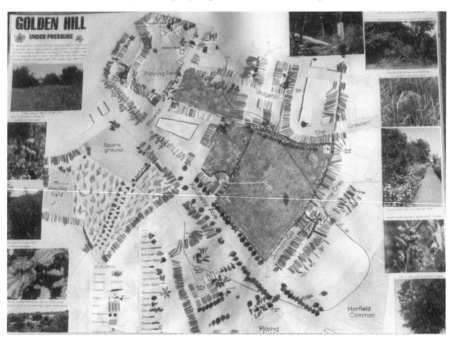

Golden Hill Map, 1987
This collage of locally found natural materials was made as a record of Golden Hill before redevelopment by Tesco. It was used in the public enquiry and at planning committee discussions and was subsequently on view at the Natural History Museum in London and elsewhere at Parish Maps exhibitions. (*Sylvia Kelly collection*)

23 December in the Watershed before the appointed inspector, Mr F. Cosgrove. A collage of locally found natural materials, buttercup petals, herbs, grasses etc was produced by Sylvia Kelly. This map was made as a record of Golden Hill before redevelopment by Tesco, planning committee discussions and was subsequently on view at the Natural History Museum in London and elsewhere at Parish Maps exhibitions.

The Inspector walked around Golden Hill on 23 December accompanied by Councillors, Council Officers, Applicants, President of HNS, Committee Members, Golden Hill Residents' Association and other local interested parties. The protesters lost this time, but some trees were saved and a group was set up to help others in similar circumstances.

1989

The Public Inquiry in respect of the outline planning application for the YMCA playing fields was held in August In December HNS urged local residents to view the plans at Brunel House and write to the Chief Planning Officer if they had objections about the proposed supermarket's layout.

1990

Executives from Tesco met local residents at a meeting. A petition signed by 3,790 people concerned about the proposed development of Golden Hill was presented to the Councillor for Horfield, Arthur Keefe, for the Avon Traffic Committee on 2 July. There was all party support to pass the planning application back to the City Council so that it could be sent on to the Secretary of State for the Environment to look at ways of revoking the decision. The YMCA offered use of its premises for a Youth Club and other Community events. Children would now be given the opportunity to participate in sports on Golden Hill.

Bristol City Council, Planning and Traffic Committee, discussed the ongoing application. They were also impressed with the collage map designed by Sylvia Kelly showing plants and wildlife on Golden Hill which had also been presented and used at the 1987 Public Inquiry.

1992

There was an Appeal in April. The next application was for a plan to cover the playing fields surrounding Tesco with 61 houses that would use the same access road as the supermarket.

1993

In spite of appeals to three Ministers of the Environment the developments went ahead in 1993. The houses, the all weather pitch and Tesco supermarket were built. However the long fight by local residents has borne fruit. Since these difficult times the Government, both National and Local, has made it virtually impossible for supermarkets to build on green field sites.

Henleaze Bowling Club

This private bowling green, unknown to many people, is located in Grange Court Road. The green was presented to the Club by the late Clarence Davey, former Sheriff of the City and County of Bristol, who resided in a large house standing on the site of the present Grange Court flats. He was Director and founder of the Metal Agencies (later known as MAC). Clubs in the City and County of Bristol Bowling Association compete annually for the Clarence Davey cup.

1928
In June 1928, when the green was opened by Lord Mayor Alderman Dowling, bowls was considered to be an old man's game, and the accommodation for players was a wooden hut.

1939
The wooden pavilion was removed and replaced by a splendidly equipped new brick building which was a gift from Clarence Davey and Charles Setter. Cars park on the site of the original pavilion.

1970–80s
Ladies were allowed to join as playing members in the 1970s and in August 1981 played and won their first club match.

2001
The Club was considered to have one of the best bowling greens in Bristol as well as fine pavilion facilities, including a licensed bar and a well-equipped kitchen.

2003
The Club celebrated their 75th anniversary in 2003.

Henleaze Lawn Tennis Club

It appears that the Tennis Club was set up in 1920 by members of the URC (now known as Trinity-Henleaze United Reformed Church). The members then were almost exclusively from the Church's Young Peoples Fellowship (YPF), the youth club.

Initially the club played on a court at Henley Grove Mansion but moved to Tennessee Grove in 1926 when the mansion was converted into apartments. Edward Corner was the Church Secretary of the URC in Waterford Road at the time of the move.

Mr Curtis of Springfield Farm sold off land in the area in 1923. He sold land to the URC church members, trustees of Westbury Park Social Club, Trinity Presbyterian Lawn Tennis Club and David Thomas Church Tennis Club. This parcel of land lay roughly between the end of Tennessee Grove and Claremont. All the tennis courts at that time were grass and there was a groundsman to look after them all.

In 2004 Don Harris (the longest serving member of Henleaze Lawn Tennis Club) advised that when he came out of the RAF in 1945 their tennis courts had been laid to tarmac.

For further information on the club please visit their website: www.henleazeltc.com

Henleaze Swimming Club

Overview

The lake and grounds are situated between Lake and Lakewood Roads. The lake is about 400 metres long and between 30–60 metres wide with a steep rock face on one side and a wooded bank on the other. About one third of the lake is used for swimming and the rest for fishing. The swimming area gives a length of just over 100 metres and an average depth of three metres, increasing to six metres under the diving area.

The wildflower species surrounding the lake include ladysmock, red campion, cranesbill, cow parsley, ox-eye daisies, hogweed, iris and water lilies. Bird life includes thrushes, blackbirds, tits, magpies, dunnocks, ducks and moorhens, with occasional visits from herons, kingfishers and cormorants.

Before 1912

The land originally formed part of a large quarry which was split into two by Eastfield Road in the nineteenth century. Limestone from these two

Henleaze Swimming Lake
Part of the former secluded Southmead Quarry which has been used for outdoor
swimming and fishing since the 1910s. (*M J Tozer collection*)

Henleaze Swimming Lake, 1930s
Aerial view looking towards Southmead which had many allotments, but few houses
then. Lakewood Road was later built to the left of the Lake. (*Henleaze Swimming Club
archives*)

quarries, then known as Southmead and Eastfield, fed five local lime kilns.

1912

Quarrying ceased in 1912 and the quarries were allowed to fill with water from springs in the sides and bottom. The ensuing expanse of water in the northern quarry became known as Southmead Lake but its name was later changed to Henleaze Lake. Major Stanley Badock (of Holmwood), the then lessee, stocked the lake with trout so that he and his friends could enjoy boating and fishing. Part of the lake was leased to a Mr Curtis who opened it for bathing. However, when a youth drowned Major Badock closed it for swimming.

1919

Albert Wain and a few friends approached Major Badock to seek permission to form a swimming club with the strict rules and regulations of the Amateur Swimming Association. This was granted and Henleaze Swimming Club was formed in May 1919. The venture was well supported and Major Badock proved to be a staunch friend and patron of the fledgling club.

The original changing facilities were very primitive; for the men a canvas screen and for the ladies a marquee, not always rainproof. Fields surrounded the lake until well into the 1920s.

Early 1920s

The original structure for the diving boards was wooden.

1924

The lake and adjoining land went up for sale by public auction and the club was unsuccessful in its attempts to purchase. Fortunately Major Badock again came to the rescue and bought it. He granted the club two successive five-year leases at a rent of £10 per annum.

1927

Major Badock was awarded his LL.D honoris causa, Doctor of Laws.

1933

Negotiations continued with Dr Badock until finally on 12 May he agreed to sell the lake to the club. Their quarters were improved and a diving tower with five, seven and ten metre boards installed with a lookout for the judges and a changing room. Originally the banks were rough and uneven and a

Skating on Henleaze Lake, 1947
The year of the big freeze. (*Henleaze Swimming Club archives*)

large stone built lime kiln existed behind the present diving stage. Much of the work was done voluntarily by club members in their spare time.

1934
During the summer, after two very dry summers and an almost rainless winter, the lake dried up leaving a few muddy pools in which hundreds of fish struggled for survival. The fish were removed and released into the River Avon and the opportunity taken to clean out the lake and remove projecting rocks. During severe winters, which have not occurred in the last fifty years, the lake would freeze over and ice-skating was a regular occurrence. The ice would have be at least nine inches thick for safety.

Before the advent of so many indoor swimming baths the lake was used for competition swimming with many international, county and local championship events being held as well as inter-club galas. Water polo was a strong feature of the club's activities with one or more matches being held every Saturday afternoon and on mid-week evenings with frequent county and international matches. Diving championships were held with displays by International and Olympic stars. Lifesaving displays were also popular. In 1930 the Club won the National Shield and many members gained RLSS awards.

1938

In 1938 the lime kiln on the site was demolished and the stone was used for filling in, reinforcing the banks as well as the toilet block.

1947

During the big freeze the lake was frozen over for several weeks so many members were also able to skate there.

1940s and 1950s

The lake was very popular and the annual gala was a big event especially the diving and water polo. The diving boards were replaced by a steel structure in the 1950s.

1960s

By the beginning of 1960 competitive swimming events and polo matches at the lake became less and less frequent. Juniors did not come up in their former numbers to replace retiring seniors and the many hours of training that increasing standards demanded were inconsistent with the cold temperatures of the lake water. However training to a high level continued with the newly dubbed Indoor Section. The club experienced hard times and by 1966 Club membership had fallen to an all-time low. No diving championships were held at the lake after 1963, and water polo at the lake ceased in 1968.

1988

In the autumn of 1988 the lake was pumped almost completely dry to allow an assessment of the fish stocks to be made and to enable rubbish to be cleared. By the following spring the springs had refilled the lake with water again. Fishing is still a feature of the lake and excellent coarse fishing is available to members.

1993

Competitive swimming and training activities were split off as a separate indoor club called Bristol Henleaze Swimming Club. Although this club conducts its activities in indoor pools the open water swimming championships are still held annually at the lake.

2006

This private club is owned by the members of the Henleaze Swimming Club and held in trust by Trustees who elect to their number (currently four in 2006) as needed. The lake is run by an Executive Committee which meets monthly. The lake, surrounded by lawns and trees is a haven of solitude for those who enjoy freshwater swimming, fishing or simply relaxing in the fresh air. Swimming, diving and sunbathing are offered from May to September. In recent years there have been some 1,350 members and there is a waiting list. Members and their guests must be able to swim at least 50 yards (46 metres). When there is work to be carried out for the club, members assist on a voluntary basis.

The all year round Fishing Section has 200 members. Fish that have been caught in the lake include carp, tench, bream, pike, roach, chubb, rudd, perch and eels.

A website is due to be launched later in 2006.

The Quarry

Mr P.W. John Clark, 1991

It is hard to visualize how the present Henleaze Park looked 60 years ago, when it was a picturesque setting for a long stretch of calm water created by the springs struck during the quarrying processes. This lake was 60–100 feet (18–30 metres) deep in places and its level was some 30 feet (9 metres) below Henleaze Road. When the lake was filled in by the Corporation the ground was brought up to road level. Rocks showing the edge of the Quarry can still be seen quite clearly in the children's playground. Changes have taken place since the following essay was written in 1933. The stables have been demolished, and the general level of the yard raised, but the weighbridge recess in Henleaze Road and the weighing bar and machinery are still there plus the lime kilns and cottage. I am trying to keep this bit of local history as authentic as possible. The cottage is reputed to be one of the oldest in Henleaze.

The Quarry Essay – John Clark, 1933

In 1916 the Quarry at the bottom of Henleaze Road (known then as Kennedy's) ceased work on account of the shortage of coal, which was used by the machinery crushing lime stone. This machinery fed two lime kilns that were situated on a level with Eastfield Road, and was used for pumping out the springs' water. After the quarrying had finished, the springs filled the place with water and then quarrying was impossible.

No one knows when the quarrying began, but some men, still living, say that they worked in it 70 years ago.

I have been told that there is also a lead mine, leading from the low level of the Quarry. The entrance to the mine is securely barred with an iron gate. Between the years 1916 and 1927 the Quarry was almost forsaken, only a few people knew of its existence. Grass, bushes and trees grew as they would around a lake.

When we arrived here in 1927 it was one of the most picturesque spots in Bristol because of the long stretch of calm spring water. The effect of the high rocks with their reflections in the water, and the different coloured leaves on the trees, made it look beautiful.

There were no fish in the lake, and although it was once stocked with 50 trout, within a few weeks they were all dead.

The stables, which were situated above the Quarry, were rebuilt about ten years ago, (circa 1923), at the expense of a Gentleman, who wanted to keep pigs on one side of the building, and a place for keeping cows on the other side, and had a high wall built to separate the lake from the pig sties.

Up to the present the only alterations made to the building have been the removal of two partitions of the pig sties and the conversion of them into a garage and the extension of the partitions in the cow shed, and the conversion of it into horse stables.

The entrance from Henleaze Road into the yard has been raised about five feet (1·5 metres), in the last five years, making it easier for the horse and motor traffic. The sheds at the bottom of the lime kilns are still in use, under which is machinery for mixing asphalt, also shelter for a motor lorry. One of the lime kilns has been filled up, but the other is still being used for a perpetual flow of gravel to feed the mixer. The office of the Quarry was one of the present bedrooms of the cottage, which had its main entrance in Eastfield Road. The pay desk pigeonhole – or the place where the weigh notes used to be handed through is still there.

When we arrived there the cottage had only two rooms downstairs, and three bedrooms upstairs, counting the one used as an office. Therefore, in our spare time, we made a hall of what had once been a chicken house and also we made a sitting room of what had once been a carriage shed, making accommodation a little larger downstairs.

The Bristol Corporation bought a large portion of the lake in May 1930 and filled it in with rubble and material that consolidated and made a hard surface.

Further information

John Clark (1916–2001) came to Henleaze as a schoolboy in 1927 and enjoyed many hours on and around the natural lake where Old Quarry Park now lies. S. Curtis & Sons, Builders, Contractors and Estate Agents ran their business here before the Clark family took over the yard and respective properties in 1927.

For over 100 years the park area was an active limestone quarry that included three lime kilns – two of which still exist in Clark's yard. Eastfield Road was extended around 1850 to bisect one very large quarry. The quarries on either side were then known as Eastfield and Southmead quarries.

1916

Rising coal prices forced the pumps to be stopped and the springs filled the quarry to give a maximum depth of 100ft (30·48 metres). In 1930 Bristol City Council purchased the land for tipping which continued for the next 20 years.

1939–45

During World War II the quarry and its water were used for training by the National Fire Service based at the junction of Hill View and Southmead Road.

From 1945

After the air raids on Bristol, rubble from the blitz damage in Central Bristol was dumped there and left to settle. The Council used part of the area as a Cleansing Station with washing and canteen facilities for road workers. Wildlife gradually arrived with self-seeded bushes and trees.

1970s

In the early '70s the Royal School for the Blind building was sold together with its playing fields and swimming pool were sold and the Council agreed to create the park for the benefit of local residents. In 1974 the quarry was levelled to form the present park with seats, swings, a small roundabout and a large climbing frame but these had deteriorated by the late 1980s.

Old Quarry Park

1990s

The Henleaze Society started to play a significant part in the improvement of the park from 1990 and Bristol City Council installed some handsome double wrought iron gates which opened up vistas and gave a more welcoming appearance to the park. About £7,000 was then contributed by The Henleaze Society for further improvements, the largest part being a gift from the proceeds of the publication of the first edition of *The Henleaze Book*.

1993

7,500 daffodil bulbs were donated by the Council and various members of The Henleaze Society assisted in planting bulbs. Bristol City Council agreed to change the name to Old Quarry Park to avoid confusion with the road Henleaze Park adjoining Henleaze Infant School. Plans for new access and pedestrian gates were drawn up in 1996 and 1997 and subsequently carried out.

2000

The Henleaze Society was awarded a National Lottery grant for £56,275 to pay for an outdoor play area and other improvements.

2001

Sunday, 15 July 2001 was the date of a landmark event in the history of The Henleaze Society. Old Quarry Park was officially opened by the well-known presenter, Sherrie Eugene, from HTV, the local ITV station and a bunch of yellow balloons (The Henleaze Society's colour) was released. Approximately 1,000 adults plus countless children attended. The afternoon centred on children and the Ambling Band, in black and pink tulle led the way. There was dancing by Miss Joyce Harper's classes, some gaily dressed as clowns; young Irish dancers in full costume; a Punch and Judy Show run by Professor Shaw; a magician, the Great Ricardo; and Novelty Scooter Races. Later, the Ambling Band gave way to a Jazz ensemble, the Swingtechs and the picnics became barbeques.

2002

The Henleaze Society received the Environmental Award from Bristol Civic Society for enhancing the environment, particularly Old Quarry Park. Over the years many members had assisted with fundraising and it was good to see their efforts rewarded for the benefit of the community. The commemorating plaque has been sited by the entrance gate.

2005

1,000 crocus bulbs were planted in the park by The Henleaze Society members in September.

Scouting

1930s

Scouting started in the 1930s in the stables of Southmead House located by the present bus stop at the bottom of Hill View (by the 1970s Georgian-style houses). Robert Powles, a founder member of the 227th Scouts (St Peter's Henleaze) recalls from the 1930s:

> The stables were used by the scouts for several years. We converted four of the loose horse boxes into dens for the patrols and in the corner was the Scoutmaster's office. We also renovated the staircase to the hayloft which we were then able to use it as a training room. Sir Stanley Badock gave us permission to use Badock Woods for events and weekend camps. We also took the Blind School scouts on annual camp, (their troop was attached to the 227th), often at East Quantockhead where we used to chop our own firewood. I recall one enthusiastic blind scout having to go to hospital after using one of the axes and cutting his leg quite badly. Fortunately he recovered quickly.

During World War II the large concrete apron of the nearby fire station was used for scout games. This fire station was subsequently demolished and replaced in the 1960s by the present one opposite the police station in Southmead Road.

1950s

The Scouts moved to St Peter's Hall in The Drive in the 1950s, for ten years, and then leased a piece of ground on the old quarry site.

In the 1950s the Scouts bought an old cricket pavilion from Brislington Cricket Club in West Town Lane. A builder was brought in to take it apart in sections. When the pavilion arrived in Henleaze it just appeared as planks of wood, so the parents and helpers set about piecing it together again.

1971

Work was started to replace the former cricket pavilion with three prefab houses (from Airport Road, Knowle) to be known as Baldwin Lodge after Geoffrey Baldwin, a former scoutmaster. The original plans were obtained before they were rebuilt and the draughtsmen designed three of everything.

1975 and 1979

Mrs Connie Baldwin opened the first and second phases on 8 February 1975 and 5 May 1979. The total cost was some £6,500. During the eight years of building no meeting was cancelled through construction work.

1991

150 young people were using the facilities each week.

Walks

Walk down Endless Lane – 1991

30 plus members attended this walk on a lovely sunny evening on 10 July. The walk started at the NatWest Bank and terminated at the Eastfield Inn. To celebrate the Society's eighteenth birthday, the then Chairman, Ron Lyne, cut a cake kindly provided by member Margaret Hosegood, formerly living in The Drive.

Beyond Endless Lane – 1992

The walk on 22 June started in Old Quarry Park, Henleaze Road and finished at the Beehive in Wellington Hill West. Highlights included a visit to Henleaze Lake and skittles at The Beehive.

Mr and Mrs John Clark joined the walk and invited members to their back garden overlooking Old Quarry Park and the former Blind School site across the other side of Henleaze Road. Walkers were also treated to a viewing of some Clark family archive photos taken in and around Henleaze during the 1920s and 1930s.

David Klemperer kindly arranged for the group to visit Henleaze Lake after normal hours when a fishing competition was in progress. Many of The Henleaze Society members had not seen the lake before and were very impressed with this unique area of quiet countryside.

The walkers continued along Glenwood Road where they encountered a swarm of wasps which a builder had disturbed whilst renovating a roof in the area. There was a brief stop at the home of one of Henleaze's former ice houses, before finishing at The Beehive for a game of skittles and a well-earned drink on what must have been one of the hottest nights of the year.

Summer Walk – 1993

The walk on 8 June 1993 started in Fallodon Court and terminated in the grounds of St Ursula's High School, Brecon Road. The route included Owen and Lawrence Groves where a fox joined the group, Cavendish and

Brecon Roads and ended with refreshments in the Balcony Room, St Ursula's Sports Hall.

YMCA Cricket Club

The YMCA Cricket Club, one of Bristol's oldest, was founded in 1878 and moved to its home at Golden Hill in North West Bristol in 1905. At its peak, in the late 1940s, the ground boasted no less than five cricket pitches that were used to support the five Saturday teams that the Club ran each week and a long wooden hut provided the changing and tea rooms. The open surroundings provided ample space for a line of mature trees that divided the two existing squares and even a duck pond that was situated near to the current score box. Many former players can recall the sight of squirrels and ducks walking onto the square on match days!

For over a century the YMCA Cricket Club has maintained their area of Golden Hill and has constantly improved the facilities including, most notably, a cricket pavilion, the foundations for which were laid in 1934 but not completed until 30 years later in 1964. Further improvements included an elaborate score box that was the envy of Bristol cricket. Such was the

Golden Hill Pavilion, 1990
This was a typical 1920 building. Its position on the highest point in the area and the clock given in memory of Bristol Grammar School old boys lost in the 1914-18 War, made it a landmark for local people. (*Sylvia Kelly collection*)

expense of the score box, the club held numerous events to raise money for the 'mechanical bicycle chain' system used to operate the display. Unfortunately, the score box burnt down one bonfire night and was replaced with the structure that stands there today. The YMCA has played a large part in the local community for over a century and many charity events have been held on its part of Golden Hill over the years. As well as the cricket club, many other local amateur sports clubs have taken advantage of the facilities in order to raise vital funds for good causes. Occasionally the ground has played host to professional teams, the most memorable of which were the YMCA benefit matches against a Gloucestershire County Cricket Club Eleven and a Bristol Rovers Football Club Eleven.

It is estimated that, during the existence of the club, over 6,000 senior and youth cricketers have represented the YMCA in thousands of cricket games, and many former members still live in the area to this day. Indeed, one of the cricket club's most respected former players was the first team captain from the mid fifties, Rev David Johnson. For further details on the YMCA cricket, please visit their website: www.ymcacricket.com/index.htm

The YMCA Cricket Club started a subcommittee in 2005 entitled 'The Golden Hill Social and Fund Raising Committee,' which included two members of the GHRA (Golden Hill Residents Association) Committee. The GHRA has set up a website www.ghra.co.uk

PART 11
FLORA AND FAUNA

Introduction

Sylvia Kelly, 1991

Long before houses were built in Henleaze there was abundant wildlife living in the considerable number of mature trees and open spaces.

Henleaze is seen today as a typical suburban district but there is a wealth of gardens. Many interested and keen-eyed residents have kept records of the unusual and tallies of the ordinary wildlife, and these have been written up for the local newsletter. Records are added to any census that is being made, whether of garden birds, butterflies, gulls or foxes.

The plateau of Golden Hill is the highest land for many miles and must be a landmark for migrating birds so Henleaze often claims the earliest and latest sightings of swifts in the city.

As it was once an area full of gentleman's residences, Henleaze also has a heritage of tree planting, both for landscaping and for botanical interest The Araucaria – Monkey Puzzle [the specimen in the grounds of Claremont] was introduced into Britain around 1851 and was almost certainly planted when the house was built, but keeled over in the January gale in 1990.

The Wellingtonia or Giant Redwood alongside was another specimen tree bringing prestige to the landowner. There are still isolated Walnuts elsewhere together with Hombeam and Oak (which may perhaps be relics of boundary marks?). The surviving Oaks are over 150 years old: the lines of Lime trees along Kellaway Avenue and the Henleaze School field boundaries are somewhat younger. There is also a Robinia (Locust Tree) in front of Henleaze Junior School and Paulownias (Foxglove Tree) at St Ursula's School and Hazels in the Manor House garden by Lake Road.

Many roads have been planted with various kinds of flowering Prunus but the street trees of a previous generation were variegated Box Elder with pretty green and yellow maple-like leaves, once used as fodder for some zoo animals. However these have not been managed properly and have mostly reverted to green, but are still neat and elegant street trees, especially in conjunction with red Maples and Copper Beech.

Our Horse Chestnuts are the fertile kind and are a source of delight to children (and parents) at conker time. When two in Holmes Grove became diseased Henleaze Neighbourhood Society planted replacements nearby – not more London Planes, which survive in spite of the bark disease which disfigures their trunks, but are really too big for this situation – but attractive Birch and Whitebeam.

There are very few suitable spaces left in Henleaze for tree planting but nevertheless Henleaze Neighbourhood Society [now The Henleaze Society] continues to raise money and press for more sites for trees to enhance the neighbourhood.

Badock's Wood

The wood comprises 14 acres (five and a half hectares) and lies in the wooded limestone valley of the River Trym between Henleaze, Southmead and Westbury. It was part of the Holmwood estate of Dr Stanley H. Badock, a local industrialist and Sheriff of Bristol from 1908 to 1909, who died in 1945. In 1937 he gave 15 acres (six hectares) of playing field and woodland to the City of Bristol, its present owners, as public open space on the condition that the city designated 15 acres (six hectares) of its own adjoining land for the same purpose. Dr Badock, it appears, envisaged the wood as a place for tree study and display.

Badock's Wood is a relic of woodland enhanced by planting with native trees such as beech, oak and ash, although the avenue of walnuts has now gone. There are hazels here indicating that this was once really old woodland here, up to 400 years old. To the north of the site, in an area of open grassland, is a Bronze Age burial mound (tumulus). The latter has been classified as 'Middle Bronze Age, constructed about 1300BC.' Today the wood is a natural oasis for wildlife bounded by urban development.

In the 1980s a nature trail, taking one hour to complete, was developed by the Badock's Wood Community Society. Birds and animals that have been seen there then included grey wagtails, chaffinches, kingfishers, wood mice, foxes, tawny owls, and hedgehogs. Look out for bluebells, forget me not, ramsons, oak, ash, beech, hawthorn and elder trees. The presence of hazel and dog's mercury indicate that this wood is a relic of ancient and probably extensive woodland.

The Friends of Badock's Wood (FOBW), in conjunction with Bristol Parks, now help by maintaining and improving the different habitats. For further information please visit their website: www.fobw.org.uk

Birds of Henleaze

Michael Smith – 1990

Watching birds in Henleaze may not seem comparable to being at Minsmere or on Fair Isle, but there are birds to be seen and heard and many come for the little food I put out for them, especially between November and April.

Many more birds fly over than I see: heron not infrequently (and once after a neighbour's new goldfish); hobby in late summer 1971 and 1980; flock of lapwing often, and curlew and redshank heard overhead at night; a flock of geese very high; mute swan quite often; mallard, pintail and teal of the ducks; swallows and house martins especially in late summer.

Numbers of gulls build up greatly in winter: black-headed feed in the garden, common aren't very common, lesser blackbacked (fewer in winter) and herring gull.

Regulars in the garden:

blackbird; blackcap (which sometimes over-winters); chaffinch (all year, but small flocks in winter); carrion crow; collared dove; dunnock; greenfinch (up to a dozen); goldcrest (and an unsubstantiated claim for a firecrest); goldfinch (small flocks); jackdaw (a flock commutes at dawn and dusk); magpie; tawny owl (still around but less common); feral pigeon (flock near Boots, Henleaze Road); recognisable individuals visit the garden; wood pigeon (maximum in hard winter); redwing (flocks regular through the winter, often with fieldfare in hard weather); robin; house sparrow; sparrow hawk (often seen, but disturbed by the builder of Tarmac Homes in Fallodon Way); starling (up to 300 in winter gatherings at tea time); swift (earliest 25 April, usually leaving roof 7–10 August); song thrush (a decline in recent years?); blue tit usual, coal, great, long tailed and willow tit less often; pied wagtail (nearest roost at Clifton Down?); garden warbler, chiffchaff and willow warbler in spring especially and wood warbler in autumn; wren.

Occasional:

bramblings (singles in autumn and spring); reed bunting (singles in winter 1981 and 1990); bullfinch; spotted flycatcher (not now for

138

several years); one immature and female pied flycatcher in autumn; mistle thrush; whitethroat (behind the Library, Northumbria Drive); great spotted woodpecker (lesser once on the Downs).'

Sylvia Kelly added that

In addition, siskin [bred in Henleaze in 2000] and green woodpecker regularly visit several gardens, hovering kestrel are seen almost every day as well as woodcock and cuckoo; there was once a hoopoe (escaped from the Zoo) bringing the grand total to 62 species. In the late 1960s tawny owls were regularly heard in the autumn. Henleaze is interpreted as meaning 'Place of the Wild Bird Wood.'

A heron was spotted twice in a garden in Oakwood Road in 1993, once taking off from a lawn and on another occasion eyeing the fishpond from a perch in a beech tree – six fish reported missing. There have been further sightings of a heron raiding fish ponds in the gardens in Southmead Road and in 2006 they were frequently seen.

Correction to the 1991 first edition from Michael Smith:

Occasional – the pied flycatcher was indeed a single bird, not two, either a female or an immature male or female.

Happily I can now add more species to the Henleaze list. In mid-September 1991 our garden was honoured by visits from a jay, exploring our carefully preserved trees. Then, in October, a careful observer reports the sighting of a siskin (species also recorded by Sylvia Kelly). The same careful observer (also a Kelly, no relation) also reported that while she was ironing she watched a grey wagtail excitedly feeding on the minute wildlife which thrives around minute goldfish pond. The adjective 'minute' applies equally to the pond and to the fish. If Sylvia Kelly can agree, on addition that makes 64 species in Henleaze?'

Sylvia Kelly reported that the first swifts of 1992 were seen over Henleaze late on 30 April.

Residents of Henleaze Gardens, Henleaze Avenue and Cavendish Road received a surprise gift in March 1995 when bird nesting boxes provided by Bristol City Council appeared in every roadside tree.

Foxes

The University of Bristol has a continuous project of studying urban foxes in our area. Whenever possible, they tag them and fit them with transmitting collars so their movements can be monitored.

In 2004, Henleaze had around ten adults in four separate groups. The population is recovering from the mange outbreak and once again the urban fox is going to be a common sight. Advice is available for people who wish to exclude foxes from their garden and the Bristol Fox Group based at the University of Bristol may also be able to assist.

Open Garden Days

The Henleaze Society has been running an Open Garden Day since 1994. In latter years it has become a biennial event and is free for members and their guests, although non-members are welcome to join the Society at the same time as they apply for tickets.

1994
Feedback from members highlighted the hidden delights and the useful gardening tips and ideas that were gleaned.

2004
A dozen gardens – large and small – were opened on Sunday, 27 June and located in three geographical groups as follows:
Upper Slopes – The Crescent – Springfield Grove
Lower Henleaze – Around Henleaze Road
Eastfield – All in Eastfield
Some of the garden owners provide collection boxes for their favourite charities and several have plants for sale as well as refreshments.

Phoenix Hedge
Sylvia Kelly 1991

Those who travel this path by the YMCA playing field daily will be interested to learn that it was officially defined as an 'access to the countryside path.' Those who object to the unkempt verges might view the nettles in a more kindly light if they realised just how many peacock and tortoiseshell butterflies, hawkmoths and other moths are reared there each summer. These beautiful creatures become scarcer each year because the plants on which their larvae feed (nettles are the most important) are so efficiently removed by officials.

Editor's note: In 1990 Henleaze Neighbourhood Society won the community prize in an environmental competition for suggesting ways of maintaining and using this site.

1992

In April it was reported that on the verges of Phoenix Hedge there were pairs of Comma, Small Tortoiseshell and Peacock butterflies, as well as red and brown ladybirds which all need nettles for their larvae.

1993

The neglect of this ancient hedge that lies between Phoenix Grove and Henleaze Park was highlighted and Avon County Council finally admitted that they were the owners and thought that it would be feasible both to restore and manage the hedge.

Strong evidence suggests that the hedge is several hundred years old as it included hawthorn, blackthorn, elm and ash trees, spindle, dogwood, elder, bramble and rose, shrublayer with rose, bryony and bittersweet. Spindle indicates a very old hedge.

It is shown on the 1881 map as a field boundary dividing two parcels of land and in those days it was properly 'laid' to keep stock enclosed.

Laying a hedge appears to be a drastic measure, but the new growth is soon apparent and makes a much healthier and thicker hedge that requires very little maintenance for another 15 to 20 years. Sylvia Kelly expressed concern over the hedge outgrowing its strength and the area thus losing a natural corridor for wildlife as well as another bit of history.

1994

Avon County Council funded half the cost of laying the 130-metre hedge and the YMCA agreed for the use of its land to burn the clippings. Keith Stuffins, a professional hedge layer worked halfway along the hedge (from Henleaze Park to the old ash tree) in mid-February, preserving trees and weaving smaller branches of thorn into a lower, but better hedge, and removing large quantities of bramble and elder. The remaining bushes responded by bursting into leaf soon after – a fitting tribute to this careful management. The rejuvenated hedge with more living branches and fewer tangles can be a corridor for wildlife again – the earliest Small

Tortoiseshells are usually seen along the path here and the number of songbirds should increase. We now have a superb example of a rural living thing in a very urban situation which will be a wonderful education resource for Henleaze Schools.

In March the new hedge was being surveyed by two pair of chaffinches, a robin, several dunnocks and bumblebees and two Small Tortoiseshell butterflies. A blackbird has since nested there.

1995

The second stage of laying was completed in March 1995, thanks to a grant from Bristol Naturalists' Society, a top up from The Henleaze Society and, most encouraging of all, sponsorship and sapling trees from many local people. Proof of the hedge's antiquity was revealed in the shape of a massive maple burr (the remains of a stump) and a large trunk of spindle. Neither of these trees is present in young hedges and both were sufficiently massive to indicate that the hedge must be at least 300 years old. The large elms at the Phoenix Grove end were also laid to encourage suckering – such shoots are more resistant to Dutch elm disease. These were only about 15 years old by a ring count. Yet another surprise emerged – two ash trees had been planted with stakes in the hedge around 1987, but there is no record of who planted them and why.

Some trees such as hazel and hawthorn were planted in the gaps in 1995 and these were carefully recorded and the information lodged with the City Museum and The Henleaze Society, so that future attempts to work out the age of the hedge by counting species will not be frustrated.

1997

Seven different berries were noted along the hedgerow:
Blackberries, sloes on the blackthorn, elderberries and purple-black clusters of berries on the dogwood, rosehip, haws on the hawthorn and scarlet berries on the climbing nightshade (bittersweet).

1999

The Henleaze Society participated in Bristol City Council's public Rights of Way 'Access for All' Survey 1999 which included surveying the 'Phoenix' footpath.

2002

Despite the proximity of Henleaze Infant and Junior Schools and Claremont School for special needs, the footpath has not been improved to accommodate prams, double buggies and wheelchairs or provide access for power-assisted wheelchairs. Nettles were cut back and some trees were removed. However verges were not resurfaced at that time and the barriers were still too closely spaced for disabled access.

Two new properties have been built on the former council canteen/store site at the Phoenix Grove end and during construction part of the hedge was decimated. However the Planning Department advised that the housing developers have voluntarily changed the fencing to allow light into the hedge to promote growth. The footpath usage has increased in the past years, particularly by shoppers, as it offers a level and quick way through from Golden Hill to Henleaze.

Wild Flowers

The following were recorded by Elizabeth Herring and Elizabeth Soloman between June and September 1996 from Kellaway Avenue to Henleaze Road via Phoenix Grove, the lane (footpath) and The Drive:

Our list is not a great one, though it represents a small triumph of nature over the forces of men in masks and white coats who cleared our roadsides and walls of every living leaf with their spray guns one day in early July, and the men who scythed the lane a little later on.

We hope you like the litany of names, many very familiar, with a few surprises.

Bittercress	Garlic Mustard
Broad-leaved Dock	Germander Speedwell
Chickweed	Goosegrass
Common Groundsel	Great Willowherb
Common Nettle	(Codlins & Cream)
Convolvulus, field & hedge	Hedge Woundwort
Corn Sowthistle	Herb Bennet
Cow Parsley	Herb Robert
Creeping Buttercup	Honesty
Cut-leaved Cranesbill	Ivy-leaved Toadflax
Daisy	Knotgrass
Dandelion	Mugwort
Dog-rose	Nipplewort
Eastern Rocket	Pineapple Mayweed
Euphorbia (Spurge)	Purple Toadflax
Field Madder	Ragwort

Shepherd's Purse
Spear Thistle
Stinking Cranesbill
Stonecrop
White Clover
White Dead-nettle
Woody Nightshade
Woody Shrubs
Bramble

Dogwood
Elder
Hawthorn
Spindle
Grasses
Bent
Rye
Wallbarley
Yellow Oat grass

PART 12
THE HENLEAZE SOCIETY

The first seeds of the Society were sewn when a few residents realised that the old Orpheus cinema was to be demolished in the early 1970s and replaced by a supermarket. The film of *The Jungle Book* had recently delighted families at half term and a local cinema seemed 'one of the bare necessities of life'. Henleaze Junior School held a debate in their top two classes 'Why must they take our cinema?' and the local media paid attention. The incorporation of the Star Cinema in the Waitrose complex in 1973 was certainly partly due to this activity.

Up until the early 1970s there had been the open-air swimming pool in the grounds of the former Blind School site. Local children had been allowed to go for a swim on summer evenings after school and, in the more relaxed atmosphere of the late sixties, whole families in the charge of an elder brother or sister would walk down there. Now the pool had been filled in and neo-Georgian houses were being built in the surrounding area. Also there was the possibility of all the trees in Cavendish Road being chopped down.

In July 1973 a group of local residents concerned about changes affecting Henleaze and the surrounding neighbourhood, arranged a public meeting in St Peter's Hall. Peter Mossman of Grange Court Road took the chair at the inaugural meeting of approximately 40 people held on 14 July 1973.

In response to the interest revealed during the meeting, Henleaze Neighbourhood Society was formed and an ad hoc committee met during the summer and produced a draft constitution. This was presented and approved, with amendments, at a public meeting on the 20 October 1973. Fifty pence per household was the agreed annual subscription. In due course the Society became a registered charity.

The Society changed its name from Henleaze Neighbourhood Society to The Henleaze Society in 1993.

In the early days of the Society membership numbers were low and did not reach 500 until the late 1970s. Since then, the Society has gone from strength to strength with the membership in 2006 reaching 1,400 households.

The Society's Objectives

The Society aims to ensure that Henleaze remains a good place to live, and is always looking for ways of improving the facilities available to the community. The areas in which it focuses its activities are:

- Monitoring planning applications and proposed developments.
- Improving parks and other open spaces.
- Trying to maintain and improve public transport.
- Supporting the continued existence of a good range of shops and businesses in Henleaze that cater for the needs of the community.
- Maintaining and improving the appearance and facilities of the shopping areas.
- Promoting and supporting the continuation of a wide range of community and leisure activities.
- Fostering a sense of community by keeping members informed of developments and activities in Henleaze.

Newsletter

A quarterly newsletter is produced and delivered by volunteer distributors to each member household in Henleaze. It provides information on a wide range of aspects of life in Henleaze, including shopping, restaurants, wildlife, local history, music, school events, recycling and the library. The newsletter received a Bristol Community Newsletter Award in 2006 for Best Delivery System.

How to Join the Society

Details are given on notice boards for details of how to join; these are located in the Library, Northumbria Drive, by the NatWest Bank in Henleaze Road and in Old Quarry Park. In 2006 the subscription is £2.50 per annum per household (or £3.50 for those who live outside Henleaze).

INDEX